THE UNIONJAC

The Unionjacking of Ireland

Jack O'Brien

MERCIER PRESS

Mercier Press Limited
P.O. Box 5, 5 French Church Street, Cork *and*
24 Lower Abbey Street, Dublin 1

© Jack O'Brien, 1993

A CIP catalogue record for this book is available from the
British Library.

ISBN 1-85635-038-X

Acknowledgements
The author and publisher gratefully acknowledge the following
publishers and individuals for their kind permission to reprint
extracts from their work in this text:
Anvil Books, Dublin, for permission to quote from *Guerrilla Days
in Ireland* by Tom Barry.
Mr Terry De Valera for permission to quote from *The Irish Republic*
by Dorothy Macardle.
Equality, The Campaign for Economic Equality, Belfast, for per-
mission to use statistics quoted in their *Directory of Discrimina-
tion*.
Gill and Macmillan, Dublin, for permission to quote from *The
Hidden Ireland* by Daniel Corkery.
Fr Joseph McVeigh for permission to quote from *A Wounded
Church*.

Printed in Ireland by Colour Books Ltd.

Contents

Dedicated to the memory of the late
Captain J.M. Feehan

Introduction

'Murder is murder is murder,' railed Mrs Thatcher at the ten IRA guerrilla fighters who lay dying in Long Kesh prison in 1980, rather than wear British prison clothes. Her contemptuous comment echoed the repeated description of the IRA of 1920 as 'a gang of criminals outside the pale of humanity'.

It was the remark of one who did not want to know anything about people struggling to get out from under foreign rule, unless it was from some rule other than British rule. Like the old man in one of Bobby Sands' stories who kept a skylark incarcerated in a cage, Mrs Thatcher tried to force her captives to sing to her tune. When they would not sing, she got angry and threw a cloak over the cage in which she held them, depriving them of their rights as political prisoners – which was like depriving them of light and air – until they were dead.

There are, however, other people who do not accept the view that the IRA are nothing more than a murder gang. Brigadier General F.P. Crozier who fought against them as Commandant of the Auxiliaries in 1920-21 was one such. In his view:

> They were not a murder gang in the correct meaning of that term but revolutionaries whose ancestors had been simmering for centuries, and who had at last become aware of the fact that in times of cut-throat upheaval necessity knows no law.

Such commentators apart, guerrilla fighters are now well aware that governments everywhere have themselves grown out of violence and that murder is part of their stock and trade. Every organisation in history – the Vatican, the

different churches, monarchies, dictatorships and protector-
ates, has murder – officially authorised murder – on its
hands. A glance through the history books tells a story of
almost continuous wars and murders. William the Conquer-
or, against the consent of the people, established the government of England at the head of a band of banditti. He
initiated hereditary succession which led to centuries of
countless murders – eight civil wars, nineteen rebellions,
scores of pitched battles, skirmishes and sieges which laid
not only England but other countries with which England
had been in conflict, in blood and ashes. His grandson,
Henry II, who initiated the conquest of Ireland, was involved in the most brutal of murders – the murder of Thomas à Becket, Archbishop of Canterbury, on the altar steps of
his own cathedral.

The above is only one example of numerous murders
committed in one country. The full list would fill volumes:
murders by the Assyrians, the Medes and the Persians,
Ulysses, Alexander the Great, Julius Caesar, Caligula, Nero,
Genghis Khan, the Turks, the Crusaders, the Borgias and the
Medici, Torquemada, the conquistadores, the Tartars, Ivan
the Terrible, Peter and Catherine the Great, Robespierre and
the Jacobins, Pol Pot and Saddam Hussein: mass murders in
tens of thousands in major events throughout history.

Every instrument of torture and every method of induc-
ing terror which the mind can conjure up, has been freely
used in these killings – scaffold, gallows, gibbet, rope, guillotine, block, rack, thumbscrew, flogging, stoning, cruci-
fixion, hanging, drawing and quartering, beheading, disem-
bowelling, fire and sword, slow burning alive at the stake,
rapid burning in urban fire storms, smothering and drowning, shooting, poisoning and gassing, radiation, starvation
and disease.

Whilst murder invariably excites revulsion and fear in
the average human it has, in some strange way, an eternal
fascination for poets, dramatists, painters and artists of all
kinds, when they are removed from the scene of the action.

Murder in a cathedral, for example, is a fearful thought

when it is associated with the murder of Archbishop Romero in San Salvador in 1980 but the presentation of T.S. Eliot's play about the murder of Thomas à Becket in Canterbury Cathedral evokes no fear because the murder took place eight hundred years ago. The murders at Troy no longer horrify because the gruesome events are immortalised in the verse of the *Iliad*. In the words of Tom Paine, 'The cruel and torturous executions, the unrelenting vindictiveness, with which more than half the Bible is filled makes it more consistent that we call it the word of a demon than the Word of God ... a history of wickedness and the greatest vices that has served to corrupt and brutalise mankind'. The murder of Macbeth, of Julius Caesar, and of thousands at Agincourt, were the outcome of sordid plots, assassinations and royal adventures in real life but in Shakespeare's plays they become the subject of sublime literary expression.

King Henry V is made to praise those who were to fight with him and lose their lives upon Saint Crispin's day, in the immortal words:

> We few, we happy few, we band of brothers;
> For he today that sheds his blood with me
> Shall be my brother;

The slaughter of six hundred common soldiers in the ill-directed charge down a valley swept by artillery fire in the battle of the Alma is romanticised into an act of great bravery in Tennyson's *Charge of the Light Brigade* – into the valley of Death and so forth. 'C'est magnifique mais ce n'est pas la guerre,' sardonically observed the French commander.

In the eyes of many British politicians, murder in Ireland has invariably been committed by rebellious natives who refused to be subjugated. As the victors saw it, Ireland had been seized to serve England's interest, and every killing that had been found necessary to maintain that interest, was justifiable and lawful. Pope Adrian IV made it clear in his Bull *Laudabiliter*, when placing Ireland within the legitimate 'sphere of influence' of England, that the Irish were 'a rude and ignorant people', and went out of his way to commend

King Henry II, for having 'set his mind upon subjugating that people', with 'splendid naval and land forces'. In the early centuries of the conquest, it was held to be 'no more sin to kill an Irishman than a dog or any other brute'.

Accordingly, in the view of many British, everything done over the centuries, in the cause of conquest, no matter how heinous, was lawful:

– 'Scorched earth' and systematic butchering, not only of men, but of women and children, by armed forces sent to subdue the island was legitimate.

– 'Anatomies of death' crawling out of the woods as described by Spenser simply meant that the wars of extermination were achieving their desired objectives.

– Starvation of 30,000 in six months of the Elizabethan wars in Munster and confirmation in the *Annals of the Four Masters* that 'from Dingle to the Rock of Cashel, not the lowing of a cow nor the voice of the ploughman was that year to be heard' were indications of the success of the authorised efforts 'to root out the Irish'.

– Sir William Cole's report on the performance of his regiment in Ulster after 1641 – 'starved and famished of the vulgar sort, whose goods were seized on by this regiment, 7000' – is no more than what was expected of him and other effective English commanders.

– Murder of children on the grounds that 'nits will make lice' was officially approved policy.

– The use of children as bucklers by Cromwell's soldiers climbing the stairs to the top of St Peter's church in Drogheda was a legitimate measure of self-defence.

– Confiscation of 11 million acres (out of a total of 20 million) under the Cromwellian Settlement and further millions under previous and subsequent confiscations indicated the totality and success of the conquest.

– Virtually halving the total population in one decade of the seventeenth century was an acceptable consequence of confiscation, and facilitated the plantation of more and more immigrant settlers.

– Annexation of the entire island in 1800 was necessary to protect the military and other interests of Britain, irrespective of the consequences for the Irish people.

– Partition of the island in 1920 was in the interest of the British political parties regardless of the wishes of the majority in the 1918 election and of the long-term damage to Ireland.

– The killing of thirteen unarmed civilians on a civil rights protest march in Derry on Bloody Sunday 1972 and dozens of other killings in Northern Ireland over recent years by forces of the Crown were all part of the continuing subjugation of the native population and the preservation of Britain's interest in that part of Ireland.

To concede such views would of course be tantamount to conceding the principle that might is right; that the rights of a weaker country can be set aside by a stronger neighbour with a lust for power and that every act of murder and terrorism committed by a conquering power in the course of conquest is lawful, and every counter-measure taken in self - defence by the country being subdued is unlawful and punishable in accordance with the aggressor's laws. If that contention were admitted in regard to Britain, then it would mean that, 'a like justification can be framed for similar acts of aggression elsewhere, and no small nation adjoining a great power could ever hope to be permitted to go its own way in peace....' That this is, nevertheless, a contention held by Britain not only about Ireland, but about her other imperial conquests as well, is evident from the remarks of the senior official in the British Foreign Office who wrote in 1936 concerning Britain's claim to the Malvinas/Falkland Islands, 'The difficulty of our position is that our seizure of the Falkland Islands in 1833 was so arbitrary a procedure that it would not be easy to explain our position without showing ourselves up as international bandits'.

Regrettably, however, the fact that they might be regarded by foreigners as international bandits never seemed to deter any of Britain's rulers from Henry II to Mrs Thatcher from seizing and holding on to what they regarded to be in Britain's interest.

1

Executed for Playing the Fiddle

The Whiteboys

By the eighteenth century the physical occupation of Ireland by Britain, which began many centuries before, was for all practical purposes complete. Organised armed resistance had ceased. Roughly 90 per cent of the land had been confiscated and placed firmly in the ownership of a small conquering minority, mostly Protestants of English or Scottish extraction and comprising less than 20 per cent of the whole population. Eleven million acres out of twenty million were planted under the Cromwellian Settlement alone and millions more under previous and subsequent settlements. Ireland was treated as just another totally subdued colony. The Protestant Ascendancy in whose care and custody it was placed, generally regarded themselves as a superior garrison in a hostile country. They were determined to exploit their newly-acquired lands for their own economic advantage in every way possible. Many of them lived abroad and left the management of their estates to agents and deputies. With notable exceptions they remained 'aliens in language, religion and blood' to the native people among whom they were settled. In the words of John Mitchel, 'For generations to come ... the subject nation, consisting of five-sixths of the population ... had no more influence upon public affairs than have the Red Indians in the United States'.

The Penal Laws

To ensure that the native people – almost entirely Catholic – dispossessed by the confiscations, could never become a threat to the new settlers, a series of laws was enacted by the colonial Parliament, with the full support of the British Government, which deprived Catholics of the most basic economic, civil, political and religious rights. They provided that no Catholic could buy land, or inherit it, or receive it as a gift from a Protestant, or lease it for more than thirty-one years, or on any lease on such terms that the profits from it exceeded one third of the rent, or raise a mortgage on it or hold a life annuity. No Catholic could own a horse worth more than £5, and any Protestant tendering that amount could claim the animal. Catholics were excluded from Parliament, from the magistracy, from the corporations, from the university, from the bench, from voting at Parliamentary elections or at vestries, from acting as constables, as sheriffs, or as jurymen, from serving in the army or navy, from becoming solicitors, or holding the office of night watchman or gamekeeper. They could not carry arms, not even a fowling piece. They could not become schoolmasters, ushers, or private tutors. Catholic children could not be educated in Irish schools except Charter schools which were at that time centres of proselytism, nor could they be sent for education abroad.

Marriage between a Catholic and a Protestant was illegal and to convert a Protestant to Catholicism was a capital offence. On the other hand if a Catholic's wife abandoned her husband's religion she was immediately free from his control and could be assigned part of his property. If any child, however young, professed itself a Protestant, it could also be assigned part of the property. If the eldest son became a Protestant he could disinherit the other members of the family, and the parent became simply a life tenant, losing all power either of selling or mortgaging the property. A Catholic could not be a guardian either to his own children or to those of another. Priests were proscribed and anyone providing shelter or protection for an unregistered priest or a banished dignitary was liable to heavy fines; for a third offence he was liable to have his goods confiscated or to lose his life as a felon. A Bill sent to England for approval in 1719 provided that unregistered priests should be castrated rather than branded on the cheek with a red-hot iron.

Those who enacted the code had small concern for Catholics' religion if only they could get their hands on Catholics' lands and goods. The assertion of the Lord Chancellor Bowes and Chief Justice Robinson from the Bench, that, 'The law does not suppose any such person to exist as an Irish Roman Catholic', sums up the attitude of the dominant minority.

Yet, these legally non-existent persons comprised roughly 80 per cent of the people. During the eighteenth century there was a fourfold increase in total population from roughly a million at the start of the century to over four million at the date of the French Revolution. Most of the Catholic population lived in the rural area and in the small centres of population – Dublin, Cork, Belfast and the bigger urban districts accounting for no more than about 10 per cent of the total. Deprived by the penal laws of the most basic human rights, they lived under atrocious conditions.

'Deputies of deputies of deputies'

The vast majority eked out a living from agriculture. They had either short leases for limited amounts of land, or were simply tenants at will on small holdings, sometimes ten or twelve acres, but more often no more than an acre or two. Nearly all were subject to rack-renting by the middlemen, described by Lecky as 'a harsh, rapacious, and dissipated class, living with an extravagance that could only be met by the most grinding exactions'. Chesterfield, when he was viceroy, commented, 'The poor in Ireland are used worse than Negroes by their lords and masters, and their deputies of deputies of deputies'.

'The system worked like a screw-press,' wrote Daniel Corkery in *The Hidden Ireland*. The increase in the rent of any farm at the close of any half-year might be small, but the screw still went on revolving, the pressure increasing until, at last, human nature could no longer endure it: agrarian outrages burst out; and on these the man-hunt followed, the noble lords blooding their young dogs. In a summary of the system, he wrote:

> The landed proprietor – the undertaker or the undertaker's descendant – would let his estate or portion of it, ten thousand acres perhaps, to a middleman: having done this, the noble lord went away to the delights of London or Bath. The middleman, renting a large house in Dublin, then became one of the crowd of place-hunters who, in the phrase of the day, spent their time in ploughing the half acre – that is, the Castle yard – keeping their eyes open, pushing their children forward, and periodically petitioning the king, through the subservient Parliament in Dublin, not to grant relief to the Catholics. The middleman usually acted as agent to a number of noble lords: impossible to oversee his far-flung and scattered acres, he in turn had recourse to men living in the various districts. These local agents, these under-agents, squireens, or stewards, usually kept an office in or near the town. They in turn again employed bailiffs to collect the rents. These bailiffs were, in many cases, renegade Gaels and renegade Catholics; they were, indeed, the actual torturers, the actual headmen under the horrible system. It was with them, and with the next nearest circle above them, the squireens, that the peasant came in contact; and the poets, who were, of course, peasants themselves, make us bitterly aware of what that contact meant for the harried people ... see these squireens as Young saw them: 'This is the class of little country gentlemen, tenants who drink their claret by means of profit rents, jobbers in farms, bucks, your fellows with round hats edged with gold, who hunt in the day, get drunk in the evening, and fight the next morning – these are the men among whom drinking, quarrelling, fighting, ravishing, etc, are found as in their native soil, once to a degree that made them the pest of society'.

There was no trick of squeezing money or value out of their tenants at will that these creatures did not know and

make use of – from the canting of farms, without a day's warning, to the cadging of poultry from the farmyards, or the jug-
gling with figures at the end of the half-year.

The peasant had to wring from the soil the gold that
supported this huge and artificial superstructure – the bailiff in
the village, the steward in the town, the agent in Dublin, the
lord in England. Living from hand to mouth, with no reserves,
the cottier was at the mercy not only of winds and rains, but of
every change, and even threat of change, in the body politic,
the body economic.

In effect, the tenant at the bottom of this pile, had to contribute to the support of up to five parasites living on his
back as well as the superior owner of the lands – the head
landlord. His rent was fixed at whatever the party immediately above him felt could be squeezed out of him. Having
no other way of living than the soil, he usually had no option but to meet the demands made on him or face eviction.
The system of annual canting under which lands were set to
the highest bidder on foot of alleged offers, made behind the
sitting tenant's back, was the ultimate in rack-renting.

There was no investment whatever by the landlord. The
tenant built his own mud dwelling and sheds for animals,
dug ditches, erected fences and planted hedges without any
security of tenure. He and his family subsisted on a diet of
skimmed milk and what was called the horse potato. Boiled
cabbages and nettles were added when available. Even in
good years many people often went hungry in July and
August when the old potatoes ran out and the new crop had
not yet come in. In bad years, when the potato crop failed,
they starved. 'Their houses and dress,' wrote Dobbs, 'were
so miserable that food was almost their only expense, and it
was computed that £10 was more than enough for the whole
annual expense of an Irish family. But the first bad year
brought them face to face with starvation. In parts of Donegal and Kerry it became the custom to bleed cattle to provide
a special dish for Sunday's dinner. The blood was mixed
with sorrel and boiled into a broth. Hence the saying, "Kerry
cows know Sunday".'

The Landlord of an Irish Estate

The relationships between landlord and tenant at the time, are graphically described by Arthur Young in his *Tour of Ireland in 1776/79*:

> The landlord of an Irish estate inhabited by Roman Catholics is a sort of despot, who yields obedience, in whatever concerns the poor, to no law but that of his will ... he can scarcely invent an order which a servant, labourer, or cottier dares to refuse to execute. Nothing satisfies him but an unyielding submission. Disrespect, or anything tending towards sauciness, he may punish with his cane or his horsewhip with the most perfect security. A poor man would have his bones broken if he offered to lift his hand in his own defence. Knocking down is spoken of in the country in a way that makes an Englishman stare ... It must strike the most careless traveller to see whole strings of cars whipped into a ditch by a gentleman's footman, to make way for his carriage. If they are overturned or broken in pieces, it is taken in patience. Were they to complain, they would perhaps be horsewhipped. The execution of the law lies very much in the hands of the justices of the peace, many of whom are drawn from the most illiberal class in the kingdom....

Shortly afterwards, that redoubtable advocate of the conquest and of the union with Great Britain – John Fitzgibbon – said in 1785, when he was Attorney General:

> I am very well acquainted with the province of Munster, and I know that it is impossible for human wretchedness to exceed that of the miserable peasantry in that province. I know that the unhappy tenantry are ground to powder by relentless landlords. It is impossible for them any longer to exist in the extreme wretchedness under which they labour. A poor man is obliged to pay £6 for an acre of potatoes, which £6 he is obliged to work out with his landlord at 5d per day ... The lower order of the people of Munster are in a state of oppression, abject poverty, sloth, dirt, and misery, not to be equalled in any other part of the world.

Tithes

In addition to having to pay exorbitant rents, tenants were also obliged to give up one tenth of their produce in tithes for the support of the pastors of the Established Church. Non-Protestant tenants were accordingly obliged to contribute to the support of the Protestant clergy as well as their own. Tithe assessments bore heaviest on the smallholders. Land for cattle grazing was exempt entirely and some graziers did very well as a result, when cattle prices rose. According to Young, 'The greatest graziers and cowkeepers perhaps in the world, some who rent and occupy from £3,000 to £10,000 a year ... the only occupiers in the Kingdom who had any considerable substance are to be found in Limerick, Tipperary, Clare, Meath and Waterford'.

A smallholder could not generally be expected to know that the exemption of pasture land from tithes was illegal, simply because it was authorised by the vote of only one House of Parliament. Even if he did know, there was little he could do about it. He could in theory bring his complaint before an ecclesiastical court but the judges in these courts would also be parties to the dispute. Those who had the monopoly of power could decide as they wished how the burden of tithes would be shared.

At one stage, tithes were raised on turf, on straw and even on furze. If the impoverished tenant was unable to pay in full he was obliged to give a bond bearing interest. 'The peasantry,' said Grattan in the course of one of the debates on tithes, 'are made tributary to the tithe farmer, draw home his corn, his hay, and his turf for nothing; give him their labour, their cars, and their horses at certain times of the year for nothing. These oppressions not only exist, but have acquired a formal and distinct appellation – tributes'.

The combined effect of exorbitant rents, tithes and other expenses was crucifying on the smallholders. Any further imposition was outside the bounds of endurance. Yet such an additional imposition occurred around 1760 when the landlords began to enclose the commons and take away the grazing rights hitherto enjoyed by the small tenants. It was the last straw. The right to graze the commons supplemented the tenants' meagre income and was a recognised part of the letting bargain without which it would have been impossible for them to pay the rents demanded. It was, however, a right based on verbal agreements and customary understandings, and when landlords, middlemen and stewards chose to ignore these, there was nothing that impoverished tenants could do to secure redress. The enclosing of the commons by the landlords at this time was motivated by the sudden rise in the value of grazing land which also led to the consolidation of many small farms and wholesale evictions. The rise in land prices was in turn the result of the rise in cattle prices which followed the removal of the embargo on Irish cattle, sheep and butter entering Britain, after a fatal outbreak of murrain had swept away vast numbers of cattle in Germany and Britain.

The chief sufferers were the smallholders rather than the bigger farmers and it was this final assault on the right of the very poor to live, which in the end, set in motion the movement described in the *Gentlemen's Magazine* for April 1762 as the Boughaleen Bawns or Whiteboys. The worms had finally turned, in the face of death by starvation.

The Worm Turns

They got their name from the fact that they generally wore white shirts over their clothes and white cockades, mainly, it would appear, to enable friend to be distinguished from foe and to facilitate maintaining contact with one another in the dark of night, which was when they usually operated. They must have presented a pretty eerie spectacle as they moved about the countryside in the dead of night, either in small parties, or when the job in hand demanded it, in large mounted parties of several hundred, levelling fences that had been erected around commonages, maiming sheep and cattle and digging up lands from which small farmers had been evicted, in order to prevent landlords from letting them for grazing.

The general aim of the movement was to obtain justice for the poor by restoring the ancient commons, and to redress grievances about tithes and other taxes. They took action against tithe proctors, tithe farmers, canters and Kerry bonds. They issued proclamations forbidding the payment of higher rents or tithes than they approved. They seized arms whenever they could and compelled all whom they suspected of connivance with the Government to abandon their farms under pain of being burnt out. A foretaste of what was now to follow had already occurred in Galway around 1715 when the ports of the continent were opened to Irish beef, and the enclosing of the commons at that time by the landlords led to such massive destruction of cattle (houghing) and other deprivations that for some years we do not hear of further enclosures.

According to Lecky, Edmund Burke maintained in an unfinished fragment, *On the Disturbances in Ireland at the beginning of the reign of George III,* that the first disturbance of the current outbreak took place in Co. Cork [*sic* Limerick]. He wrote:

A very respectable Protestant attorney named Fant was living, in 1760, on the borders of that county, and he had for a long time enjoyed a good reputation. His mind, however, gradually became disordered. He entered into a long succession of disputes with his neighbours, and at last finding some charges he had made against them disregarded by the Government, he shortly after the arrival of Lord Halifax [October 1761], assembled many of the meaner people of Kilmallock, and having warmed them with liquor, he harangued on the grievances which the poor in general suffered from the oppression of the rich, and telling them their town common had been illegally enclosed, and that they had a right by law to level the walls by which they were shut out from it, they very readily engaged under the authority of a lawyer, and that night completely demolished all the fences which enclosed their reputed common.

Some nine months later (June 1762), Wesley was travelling through Ireland and is said to have taken great pains to obtain accurate information about the movement. In his *Journal,* he states:

About the beginning of December last [1761] a few men met by night near Nenagh, in the county of Limerick [*sic* Tipperary],

and threw down the fences of some commons which had been
lately enclosed. Near the same time, others met in the counties
of Tipperary, Waterford, and Cork. As no one offered to suppress or hinder them, they increased in numbers continually,
calling themselves Whiteboys, wearing white cockades and
white linen frocks. In February there were five or six parties of
them, 200 to 300 men in each, who moved up and down chief-
ly in the night ... levelled a few fences, dug up some grounds,
and hamstrung some cattle, perhaps fifty or sixty in all. One
body of them came into Clogheen, of about 500 foot, and 200
horse. They moved as exactly as regular troops, and appeared
to be thoroughly disciplined. They sent threatening letters,
compelled every one they met to swear allegiance to their leader, 'Queen Sive', and to obey her commands, and threatened
savage penalties against those who refused to do so.

Wherever the first outbreak occurred, it is clear that the
movement spread rapidly throughout Cork, Limerick, Tipperary and Waterford, and a number of Munster towns –
Newmarket, Kilworth, Mitchelstown, Clogheen and Clonmel – are mentioned in separate accounts given by Lecky. In
one of these he states that:

In some cases the Whiteboys acted with all the audacity of
open insurgents. Great bodies of men traversed the country,
often in the open daylight, wearing white cockades and blow-
ing horns. In several cases they awaited an encounter with
soldiers. They broke open the jail at Tralee and released the
prisoners. They threatened to burn the town of Newmarket ...
unless a Whiteboy confined there was released. They burnt
several houses which soldiers had occupied ... On one occasion, a large party, well mounted and clad in white, rode into
the little town of Kilworth, in the county of Cork, at three in
the morning, firing many shots, and compelled the inhabitants
... to illuminate their windows, which was done speedily and
in great order, more from fear than respect.

In another account, he states:

As early as 1762 an informant writes from the county of Tipperary that 'above 500 men frequently assemble with shirts
over their clothes doing whatever mischief they please at
night, under the sanction of being fairies, as they call themselves ... The fairies are composed of all the able young fellows

from Clonmel to Mitchelstown.' They had levelled great numbers of enclosures, sent many threatening letters, rescued property which had been seized by landlords for non-payment of rent, compelled cloth weavers to lower the price of their goods, seized all the horses they could discover around Cahir, and established such a terrorism in the county that if any farmer dismissed a servant or a shepherd no one dared take his place unless 'he had more interest with the fairies'. No one was allowed to bid for a farm which had been put up to auction until it had been waste for five years on pain of death or the burning of his house. Grass land was sometimes turned up to oblige the landlord to let it for tillage, and great numbers of cattle were killed or hamstrung ... The exportation of corn and flour was sometimes obstructed by force, masters were compelled to release their apprentices, daughters of rich farmers were carried away and forced into marriage, sums of money were levied from farmers to defend the Whiteboys on their trial. In some districts large bodies of men appeared on market day on the roads round some country town, or on Sundays near the chapel doors, compelling all who passed to swear that they would obey the laws of Captain Right.

All of the accounts convey the impression of a loosely-organised disciplined body, something on the lines of the minute men in the American colonies, capable of mounting speedy counter-attacks against enclosures, impounding of livestock, canting of farms and other actions of landlords which adversely affected them. The oath taken by members shows that they understood the importance of co-operation, secrecy, speed and loyalty to one another, and suggests some acquaintance with military operations

Whiteboy Rule and Landlord Reprisals

Where they were well organised they were sufficiently strong to be able to enforce their rule. Few murders are attributed to them but many less drastic measures could be and were taken against informers and against people who refused to obey their unwritten laws against bidding for farms already tenanted (canting), or bidding for farms at auctions which had been boycotted, or purchasing livestock seized by bailiffs in distraint of rent and other matters. For such offences it would appear that offenders were as a minimum seized and compelled to swear that they would never repeat the offence, or in more serious cases, dragged from their beds at night, beaten up, bound and left naked in a ditch by the roadside, or brought to a newly-dug grave where they were left buried up to the chin in earth, thorns or furze, or placed naked on horseback and forced to ride a distance on saddles covered with thorns or a hedgehog's skin or glass. Cottages of culprits were sometimes burnt out and occupants forced to leave the area. In one reported case an offender was bound to the post of a turnpike gate and the keeper was compelled to swear that he would not relieve him until a certain time had passed. Cutting off of ears was a common punishment.

Davitt writes that by such methods, the Whiteboys:

> ... terrorised grabbers, graziers, and other landlord supporters, and enforced their decrees by such powers as secret combination gave them ... In this manner they gave some protection to a peasant's life and labour, which neither the Government nor the law in the hands of the landlords would offer, and Whiteboyism, though guilty of many acts of cruelty and of unnecessary violence, struck the first blow in Ireland at the rampant tyranny of Cromwellian landlordism by asserting the superior right of the people ... The law denied the people almost all civilised rights, and made the interests and protection of landlord property the only care or concern of civil government. The least infringement of this law meant years of savage imprisonment, and frequently death for the accused. The life of a sheep or of a pheasant was of more value in the eye of such a law than the life of a human being. Rent was the supreme end of land tenure. The soil existed for no other purpose.

The savage punishments meted out to Whiteboys whenever one was brought to trial bear out the truth of these remarks. Five men were executed at Waterford in 1762 'for having been present at the burning down of a cabin, upon the information of one their associates, who was the very person that with his own hand set fire to it'.

On Wednesday, 9 June 1762, according to a subsequent chronicle of events in the *Gentleman's Magazine*, 'the trials of the Levellers ended, when three of the ringleaders were ordered for execution, viz, Pierce Burley, for breaking into the house of Mr Montgomery, and taking thereout bacon and other eatables; Robert Stackpoole (who acted as captain) for killing a bay gelding, by shooting and barbarously beating him, because the property of James Grove, Esq, who had been active in suppressing the Levellers; and Pierce Moore, for being present, and playing on the fiddle at the killing of the said horse. The judges, at the request of the grand jury, ordered the execution of these three convicts to be as near as possible to the places where the outrages have been committed, in hopes of deterring others from involving themselves in the like distress for the future.'

Fr Nicholas Sheehy – The Whiteboy Priest

There were hundreds of other murders, 'trials' and executions but the judicial murder of Fr Nicholas Sheehy of Clogheen probably best demonstrates the temper of the day and the determination of the colonial landlords and their supporters to wreak their revenge on the Whiteboy movement – through the person of a prominent Catholic pastor – in the area of its greatest activity.

Clogheen is a small village nine miles east of Mitchelstown in a valley between the Galtees and the Knockmealdown mountains and half way between Mitchelstown and Clonmel. Its parish priest in the 1760s was Fr Nicholas Sheehy, a young man born in Fethard – about six miles north of Clonmel – and educated on the continent. He was an outspoken opponent of the levying of tithes on Catholic parishioners for the support of the Protestant clergy.

In the adjoining parish of Newcastle where there were no Protestant parishioners, he claimed that no tithes should be paid, and the people refused to pay them. In the area of Ballyporeen, some three miles from Clogheen, a tithe proctor named Dobbyn made a claim upon the Catholics of five shillings for every marriage celebrated by a priest, on behalf of two Protestant clergymen – Messrs Foulkes and Sutton. The

claim was resisted by the people, who were parishioners of
Fr Sheehy, and he denounced it publicly. He furthermore
questioned the right of the Protestant clergy to tithes from a
people for whom they provided no care.

That a Catholic pastor should presume to claim rights
on behalf of people who, according to the learned Lord
Chancellor Bowes and Chief Justice Robinson, the law does
not suppose to exist, was more than the Cromwellian magistrates and Anglican rectors of Munster were prepared to
tolerate. They resolved to have his blood.

When the Whiteboy troubles broke out in Munster in
1762 the Marquis of Drogheda was sent to Clogheen with a
considerable military force to 'pacify the country round
about'. Great numbers of 'insurgents' are stated to have been
killed in this 'pacification' exercise, but it is not stated what
they were doing when they were killed, nor are we told the
exact nature of the insurrection. According to Edmund
Burke, there was no insurrection or Popish plot or association with any foreign power as alleged. Nevertheless, the
troops were let loose on the countryside and given free reign
to suppress the imaginary insurrection with the assistance
and guidance of distinguished local gentlemen like Sir
Thomas Maude, William Bagwell and John Bagwell Es-
quires, and others, who daily accompanied the military on
their operations. Many arrests were made as well as murders committed. Preparations were made for the indictment
of those arrested before juries of their mortal enemies em-
panelled by Daniel Toler, high sheriff of the county and
either father or uncle of that other Toler, the bloody judge
known to history as Norbury.

No Roman Catholic leader of any respectability could be
found to give credibility to the rumour of a Popish insurrection. Accordingly, the parish priest of the village – Fr Sheehy
– had to be suspected of disaffection. He had collected money for the defence of some of the rioters who were his parishioners, and the acquittal of many of them was attributed
to his interference. He was arrested and indicted several
times but the charges always failed for lack of evidence.

At Clonmel General Assizes, 23 May 1763, he and others were charged with unlawful assembly, assaulting William Ross and compelling him to swear that he would never disclose anything to the prejudice of the Whiteboys. At the Summer Assizes of 1764 he was again indicted along with others of assaulting John Bridge. He had already been examined on the same charge the previous year and let go free because of lack of evidence. Following examination under torture, Bridge, himself a Whiteboy, had come out with allegations against some of his former colleagues, including Fr Sheehy. These men were charged with having been amongst the rioters who had assembled near the town on the night of the day Lord Drogheda arrived at Clogheen. In October 1763, Bridge disappeared and, although his body had not been found, a report was circulated that he had been murdered by the Whiteboys. Between the date of his disappearance and the spring of 1764, Sheehy was constantly menaced with prosecution; witnesses were frequently examined and indictments framed, but no criminal proceedings followed. He was forced to go into hiding.

At length, the Government was persuaded to issue a proclamation against him in 1765, in which he was described as a fugitive from justice, charged with high treason, and offering £300 for his apprehension. Sheehy immediately offered to surrender himself provided he was tried in Dublin rather than Clonmel where the malice of his enemies would prevent him getting a fair trial. His offer was accepted and on 10 February, in the following year, 1766, he was brought to trial in the Court of King's Bench. The indictment charged him with acting as a leader in a treasonable conspiracy, exercising men under arms, swearing them to allegiance to the French king, and inciting them to rebellion. The witnesses produced were a man named John Toohy who, a month previously, had been committed to Kilkenny jail on a charge of horse-stealing, a prostitute named Mary Butler and a vagrant boy named Lonergan, the latter two brought from Clonmel jail and bribed to testify against him. After a fourteen-hour trial he was acquitted.

However, his enemies were not to be denied their prey. Immediately after his acquittal, the Chief Justice informed him of a fresh charge of murder, and on this charge he must be committed to Newgate. After two or three days in prison he was handed over to his persecutors and brought back to Clonmel to stand trial before his bitterest enemies. He was conveyed on horseback under a strong military escort, with his arms pinioned and his feet tied under the horse's belly.

On 12 March 1766, he was put on trial in Clonmel for the murder of John Bridge, the Whiteboy who had turned informer. In the indictment he was charged with having been present at and aiding and abetting Edmund Meighan in the said murder, and with having proposed the murder of him and of Lord Carrick, John Bagwell, William Bagwell and other persons obnoxious to them, at an assemblage of Whiteboys in the house of his sister, Mrs Green of Shanbally near Clogheen, and with swearing all those present to secrecy, fidelity to the French king, and the commission of the proposed murders. Most of the witnesses who gave evidence at his former trial were produced again on this occasion. Among the new witnesses was a woman of abandoned character known as 'Moll Dunlea' and introduced at the trial as Mrs Mary Brady, the latter being the name of a soldier of the light horse, with whom she then cohabited.

The 'trial' was so managed that the witnesses whom Fr Sheehy could have produced were unable to give evidence. A reliable witness named Keating was prepared to testify that on the night of the supposed murder the accused was in his house and could not have been present at the murder, but the Reverend Mr Hewetson, an active manager at the trial, stood up and informed the court that he had Mr Keating's name on his list as one of those that were concerned in the killing of a corporal and sergeant in an earlier rescue of some of these levellers. Keating was thus debarred from giving evidence, and was in fact hurried away to Kilkenny jail to face trial himself at a later stage. He was acquitted of the charge brought against him, but the accusation of the Reverend Hewetson at Clonmel had the effect of depriving Fr

Sheehy of the testimony of his most essential witness. It also had the effect of frightening off others who came to give evidence, lest they meet with the same treatment.

It made no pretence to be anything other than a mockery of a trial but it was expedient that Fr Sheehy be found guilty and executed. He was accordingly condemned to be hanged, drawn and quartered. The sentence was carried out in Clonmel on 15 March 1766. His head was stuck on a spike over the porch of the old jail where it remained for twenty years until his sister was permitted to take it away for burial with his body in the old churchyard at Shandrahan. He was thirty-eight.

'A Most Foul Conspiracy'

On Saturday, 3 May 1766, three more persons of credit – Edmund Sheehy, James Buxton and James Farrell – were hanged, drawn and quartered at Clogheen after conviction in Clonmel of being involved in the murder of Bridge, on the admittedly perjured evidence of two prisoners who swore away the lives of the accused, in order to save their own. Mitchel wrote:

> The whole of these military executions and judicial trials in Munster, extending over four years were themselves the result of a most foul conspiracy on the part of the Ascendancy faction, with its Government, its judges, its magistrates, and its juries – based upon carefully organised perjury and carried through by brute force, to 'strike terror' in Tipperary, to destroy all the leading Catholics of that troublesome neighbourhood; and above and before all things, to hang and quarter the body, and spike the head, of the generous and kindly priest who told his people that they were human beings and had rights and wrongs.

Instead of endeavouring to redress the matters which had caused the Whiteboy outbreak in the first instance and which continued to sustain the movement, the landlord-dominated Parliament simply continued to enact repressive legislation, designed to suppress totally all semblance of agrarian revolt. By an Act of 1765, all persons who went by night in parties of five or more men, wounding, beating, tying up, or otherwise assaulting human beings, destroying property, or digging up ground, all who were engaged in breaking open jails or rescuing felons, and all who imposed unlawful oaths of violence were made liable to death. The grand juries were empowered to levy on the barony in which a crime was committed a sum to compensate the injured person, unless the offenders were given up, or unless some evidence was given against them. Another clause provided that any magistrate could summon before him any persons whom he suspected of having taken an illegal oath, examine them, and imprison them for six months if they refused to answer.

Ten years later, the Whiteboys were still active in Munster trying by violence and intimidation to resist tithe proctors and tithe farmers, to raise wages and lower rents and dues. The response of Parliament then, was to enact still another Crimes Act which, as well as re-enacting the punitive measures of the earlier legislation and creating some new misdemeanours, greatly added to the list of capital offences. Among these were publishing a Whiteboy notice, maiming or disfiguring human beings, sending threatening letters, compelling men to quit their farms, habitations, or employments, or to join in Whiteboy offences, entering houses by force or menace between sunset and 6 a.m. in order to take horses, weapons, or money, or assisting or concealing Whiteboys who had committed any capital offence.

The Bill was opposed by Curran but supported by Grattan, so much was he afraid of the Whiteboy threat to property and the established order. He subsequently introduced a motion to inquire into the subject of tithes and to form a plan for the support of the clergy. The motion was defeated and the people were left as heretofore to the mercy of tithe proctors, tithe farmers, clergy and landlords.

Although the military executions and the repression following the foregoing enactments naturally forced some curtailment of openly-organised activities, the Whiteboy spirit was never really suppressed because the oppression which gave rise to the movement in the first instance was not relaxed but rather aggravated. Tithes were not abolished until 1838 and then only to the extent of being merged in the rent. Unlike the United Irishmen and subsequent armed political organisations fighting for freedom from British rule, the Whiteboy movement was essentially an unarmed agrarian confederacy of the grievously oppressed rural poor, whose aim was confined to improving their material lot, and lasted under one name or another until landlordism itself came to an end at the turn of this century.

Lord Charlemont, chief commander of the Volunteers, though strongly anti-Catholic in his views, understood the real causes of Whiteboyism. They were, he said:

> exorbitant rents, low wages, want of employment, farms of enormous extent let by rapacious and indolent proprietors to monopolising land-jobbers, by whom small portions of them were again let and re-let to intermediate oppressors and by them sub-divided for five times their value among the wretched starvers upon potatoes and water; taxes yearly increasing, and still more tithes, which the Catholic, without any possible benefit, unwillingly pays in addition to his priest's money; ... misery, oppression, and famine.

This assessment was fully corroborated by Dr Madden.

'Man's natural right and duty to rebel'

Lord Chesterfield seemed not to have any qualms about the barbarities of the rural 'Jacquerie', as Dr Madden termed them, and ascribed Whiteboyism to 'the sentiment in every human breast that asserts man's natural right to liberty and good usage, and that will and ought to rebel when oppressed and provoked to a certain degree'. Being well aware, as he had already proclaimed, that tenants in Ireland 'were used worse than Negroes by their lords and masters', he went so far as to say that, if the military had killed half as many landlords as they did Whiteboys they would have contributed more effectively to restore quiet.

Arthur Young and the Domineering Aristocracy

Ten years after Fr Sheehy of Clogheen had been hanged,
drawn and quartered in Clonmel, and while his parishioners
could still behold his blackening skull withering away on
the spike over the old jail, an Englishman came to work as
agent for the biggest landlord in the area – Robert King,
Lord Kingsborough, later second Earl of Kingston. He was
Arthur Young, who had travelled extensively throughout
Ireland during the previous two years and was a noted
authority on Irish affairs at that time. Young's account of the
conditions under which the common people of the area lived, explains why Whiteboyism was rampant from Kilmallock to Clogheen and further afield:

> The immense property was in the hands of that species of
> tenant ... which in Ireland has flourished almost to the de-
> struction of the Kingdom, the middleman, whose business and
> whole industry consists in hiring great tracts of land as cheap
> as he can, and re-letting them to others as dear as he can ... the
> agent employed to manage the estate during Lady Kings-
> borough's minority visited it no more than once or twice a year
> ... he employed a clerk whose office was in a summerhouse in
> the castle grounds whither tenants came to pay their rents ...
> the property has been denuded of trees and in an estate of over
> a hundred thousand acres you must take a breathing gallop to
> find a stick large enough to beat a dog ... labour is chiefly done
> under the cotter system; there are here every gradation of the
> lower classes, from the spalpeen, many among them strangers,
> who build themselves a wretched cabin in the road, and have
> neither land, cattle nor turf, rising to the regular cotter, and
> from him to the little joint tenant, who united with many
> others, takes some large farm in partnership: still rising to the
> greater farmer ... the population is very great ... the cabins are
> innumerable, and like most Irish cabins swarm with children
> ... hogs are kept in such numbers that the little towns and vil-
> lages swarm with them; pigs and children bask and roll about.
> I believe that there are more pigs in Mitchelstown than human
> beings and yet propagation is the only trade that flourished
> here for ages ... in my rides around Mitchelstown I have pass-
> ed places in the road one day without any appearance of a ha-
> bitation, and next morning found a hovel, filled with a man
> and woman, six or eight children and a pig ... Mitchelstown
> was a den of vagabonds, thieves, rioters and Whiteboys.

Mitchelstown Estates comprising over one hundred thousand acres, stretched from Kilmallock to Clogheen and were in feudal ownership for over five hundred years from the time King Henry III made the original grant to Gilbert, the first White Knight, by letters Patent dated 1270. The owner in Young's time – Robert King – was descended from a King family which came to Ireland in the days of Queen Elizabeth and settled in Boyle, Co. Roscommon. He came into possession of the Mitchelstown Estates through marriage in December 1769 to his cousin Caroline Fitzgerald, sole heiress and successor to the White Knight. She was aged fourteen and he was fifteen. The lands at Mitchelstown had to be held in trust until the heiress came of age in 1776 when the twenty-one-year-old couple – now with four or five children – took up residence at Mitchelstown Castle. Robert was also heir to his father's lands and titles in Roscommon and the combined properties put him among the biggest landowners in Ireland. Prior to his marriage he was attending school at Eton. He was actually withdrawn for the wedding and finished his education at home under a private tutor. When the wedding was over, he took his fourteen-year-old wife to live in his father's town house at 15/16 Henrietta Street; thence to a rented house in London and thereafter on a grand tour of the continent. As Disraeli remarked a century later about England, 'the Privileged and the People formed Two Nations'.

Kingsborough was an immensely wealthy landowner, but he never had the slightest contact with the thousands of helots, whose unremitting toil produced that wealth. They lived like slaves on his vast estates, without education, adequate food or clothing, or even the most basic human rights. Six miles of a ten-foot-high limestone wall, surrounding the thirteen hundred acres of demesne lands in the precincts of the castle, which he retained for his own private farming, kept the two worlds apart. All the rich and fat things of the universe were for the enjoyment of the landlord and his family within the demesne. Any assault on that world by tenants or Whiteboys was to be suppressed without a thought by bailiffs and the military.

Young knew the Kingsborough set-up thoroughly, and he was also well acquainted with many other landlords in the disturbed parts of Munster such as the Aldworths of Newmarket – another main centre of Whiteboy activity – the Bowens of Bowen's Court and others. He described them all collectively as, 'The domineering aristocracy of 500,000 Protestants [who] feel the sweets of having two millions of slaves'.

The Whiteboys achieved some successes against rack-renting, excessive tithes, canting and similar injustices, but they did not shift or even dent Irish landlordism. It would have taken an armed revolution at that time – as in France twenty years later – to undo the grip on the country, achieved by the almost universal confiscations and the all pervasive penal laws. The common people had no arms with which to confront the arms of the landlords and the military. The actions open to them, therefore, were such only as could be taken by an unarmed people.

The landlords' castles and big houses built out of the rack-rents extracted from the oppressed people of the seventeenth and eighteenth centuries have disappeared one by one in the present century. Mitchelstown Castle went up in fire and flames on 12 August 1922, during the civil war. The Aldworths left Newmarket in the early 1920s, and their home became a convent. Bowen's Court was sold by its last owner, Elizabeth Bowen the writer, in 1959, and razed to the ground shortly afterwards. All are now no more than local historical memories. The grave of the martyred Whiteboy priest, Fr Nicholas Sheehy, at Shandrahan is, however, still a place of constant pilgrimage.

2

'Man is born free'

The United Irishmen

PART 1: A Nation of Slaves

While the Whiteboys were struggling in rural Ireland for the barest of material needs – the right of poor people to sufficient food to feed themselves and their families – radical thinkers in other parts of the world were busy promulgating revolutionary ideas about political and religious freedom which would shortly shake Europe and America to their foundations. Starting with the assertion that 'Man is born free, and everywhere he is in chains', Jean-Jacques Rousseau published his treatise *Du Contrat Social*, urging 'Liberty, Equality and Fraternity' for all; Tom Paine proclaimed that 'Freedom hath been hunted round the globe', and asked those 'that dared oppose, not only tyranny but the tyrant to stand forth'; and Jefferson wrote the memorable words: 'all men are created equal ... from that equal creation they derive rights inherent and inalienable, among which are ... life, and liberty, and the pursuit of happiness'.

In Ireland, however, the political and economic status of roughly three million people had not advanced beyond the miserable position grudgingly conferred by the Bogland Act of 1771 which enabled Catholics to take leases for sixty-one years on no more than fifty acres of unprofitable land, and the Gardiner Relief Act of 1778 which extended the concession, subject to a humiliating oath of allegiance to a foreign king. Rural people generally knew nothing about their God-given rights, and poor Catholic peasants, accustomed to appalling poverty and exploitation were being told by their clergy and civil authorities to remain quiet and be thankful for small mercies from their subjugators and their masters. An urban merchant class which grew rich, mainly out of grazing and the provision trade, and a Catholic Committee concerned with civil rights for upper and middle classes, began to thrive in the improved conditions which followed the gradual relaxation of the penal code. The condition of the vast majority – the rural proletariat – remained, for all practical purposes, unchanged.

Who are the People?

News about what was happening abroad after the American and French Revolutions was published regularly in the *Freeman's Journal* and other papers, but circulation of these papers was limited. There were also a number of political clubs in the main cities – Whig Clubs, Constitutional Clubs, Societies for the Preservation of Peace – where certain ideas acceptable to them could be discussed, but subjects which were not to their taste could not be discussed at all. The influence of such clubs outside their own narrow circles was negligible. At the time the United Irish Society was formed, it was the only association of any kind which even admitted a Catholic into its ranks.

No Catholic could be in the Whig Club, nor would it permit the Catholic question to be discussed. At a meeting of the club, held a full year after the founding of the United Irish Society, one member went so far as to say that if the Catholic question were admitted to be debated, he would with his own hand strike his name out of the list of members. On the other hand, Hamilton Rowan replied that he would not hesitate to strip off his Whig Club uniform and throw it to the waiter, if the Catholic question were deemed an unfit subject for their discussion. Another member – Mr Brown – called attention to the purpose of their association. 'They placed themselves,' he said, 'in the front of the public cause, to further it, not to stop its further progress; the second principle of their declaration was a solemn engagement to support the rights of the people, etc'. He then asked, 'Who are the people? I dare any gentleman to name the people of Ireland without including the Roman Catholics. What! is it a question? Shall three millions of Irishmen continue slaves or obtain their freedom! Is a question to be deserted by men professing patriotism, professing to redress the public oppression, pledged to stand together in defence of their country's liberties? No; it is not'.

The Society of United Irishmen

It was against this background that a new Political Club was established in Belfast in 1790 by a small secret committee of eleven Presbyterian businessmen. As yet it had no name. In September 1791, a pamphlet published in Dublin under the signature of 'A Northern Whig', and entitled, 'An argument on behalf of the Catholics of Ireland', came to their notice. It expounded ideas similar to their own. They got in touch with the author who turned out not to be a Northern Whig but a young Dublin barrister, 'a Protestant of the Church of Ireland named Theobald Wolfe Tone', who also happened to be a close friend of one who had been an associate member of their club while he was an officer of the British army stationed in Belfast the year before – one Thomas Russell. They invited both to Belfast for a discussion and it was this meeting which led within days to the founding of a new society on 14 October 1791, which they called the Society of United Irishmen. It was an entirely constitutional and legal organisation formed as stated in the first sentence of its constitution, 'for the purpose of forwarding a brotherhood of affection, a communion of rights, and a union of power among Irishmen of every religious persuasion, and thereby to obtain a complete reform in the legislature founded on the principles of civil, political, and religious liberty'.

The society's Dublin branch was founded three weeks later in the Eagle Tavern at 3 Eustace Street. As a commentary on the time, the minutes of that meeting, signed by the Secretary, James Napper Tandy, are worth quoting in full:

Society of United Irishmen, Eagle Tavern, Eustace Street, 9 November 1791. At a meeting of the Society of United Irishmen of Dublin, The Hon. Simon Butler, in the Chair, the following was agreed to:

When we reflect how often the freemen and freeholders of Dublin have been convened, bluntly to express their grievances to Parliament – how often they have solicited the enaction of good, and the repeal of bad Laws – how often, for successive years, they have petitioned against the obnoxious – and unconstitutional Police Act, and how often all these applications have been treated with the most perfect contumacy and contempt – when these facts are brought to recollection, is there an honest man will say that the House of Commons have the smallest respect for the People or believe themselves their legitimate representatives? The fact is, that the great majority of that House consider themselves as the representatives of their own money, or the hired servants of the English Government, whose Minister here is appointed for the sole purpose of dealing out corruption to them – at the expense of Irish liberty, Irish commerce and Irish improvement. This being the case, it naturally follows that such Minister is not only the representative of the English views against this Country but is also the sole representative of the people of Ireland. To elucidate which assertion, it is only necessary to ask, whether a single question in favour of this oppressed nation can be carried without his consent? – and whether any measure however inimical, may not through his influence be effected?

In this state of abject slavery, no hope remains for us, but in the sincere and hearty union of all the people, for a complete and radical reform of Parliament; because it is obvious that one party alone have been ever unable to obtain a single blessing for their country; and the policy of our rulers has been always such as to keep the different sects at variance in which they have been but too well seconded by our own folly.

For the attainment then of this great and important object – for the removal of absurd and ruinous distinctions – and for promoting a complete coalition of the People – a Society has been formed, composed of all religious persuasions who have adopted for their name – The Society of United Irishmen of

Dublin – and have taken as their Declaration that of a similar society in Belfast which is as follows:

In the present great era of reform when unjust Governments are falling in every quarter of Europe; when religious persecution is compelled to abjure her tyranny over conscience; when the Rights of Men are ascertained in theory, and that theory substantiated by practice; when antiquity can no longer defend absurd and oppressive forms against the common sense and common interests of mankind; when all government is acknowledged to originate from the People and to be so far only obligatory as it protects their rights and promotes their welfare; we think it our duty, as Irishmen, to come forward and state what we feel to be our heavy grievance and what we know to be its effectual remedy.

We have no National Government. – We are ruled by Englishmen and the servants of Englishmen; whose object is the interest of another country and whose instrument is corruption; whose strength is the weakness of Ireland; and these men have the whole of the power and patronage of the country as means to seduce and subdue the honesty and the spirit of her representatives in the legislature. Such an extrinsic power, acting with uniform force in a direction too frequently opposite to the true line of our obvious interest can be resisted with effect solely by unanimity, decision, and spirit in the people – qualities which may be exerted most legally, constitutionally and efficaciously by that great measure, essential to the prosperity and freedom of Ireland, an equal representation of all the people in Parliament.

We do not here mention as grievances the rejection of a place-bill, of a pension bill, of a responsibility bill; the sale of Peerages in one House; the corruption publicly avowed in the other; nor the notorious infamy of Borough traffic between both; not that we are insensible of their enormity but that we consider them as but symptoms of that mortal disease which corrodes the vitals of our constitution and leaves to the people in their own government but the shadow of a name.

Impressed with these sentiments we have agreed to form an association to be called The Society of United Irishmen; and we do pledge ourselves to our country, and mutually to each other, that we will steadily support, and endeavour by all due means to carry into effect the following resolutions:

1. Resolved that the weight of English influence in the government of this country is so great as to require a cordial union among all the people of Ireland, to maintain that balance which is essential to the preservation of our liberties and the

extension of our commerce.

2. That the sole constitutional mode by which this influence can be opposed is by a complete and radical reform of the representation of the people in Parliament.

3. That no reform is practicable, efficacious, or just which shall not include Irishmen of every religious persuasion.

Satisfied as we are, that the intestine divisions among Irishmen have too often given encouragement and impunity to audacious and corrupt administrations, in measures which but for these divisions they durst not have attempted, we submit our resolutions to the nation as the basis of our political faith.

We have gone to what we perceive to be the root of the evil. We have stated what we conceive to be the remedy. With a Parliament thus reformed, everything is easy; without it nothing can be done. And we do call on, and most earnestly exhort our countrymen in general to follow our example and form similar societies in every quarter of the kingdom for the promotion of constitutional knowledge, the abolition of bigotry in religion and politics, and the equal distribution of the rights of man throughout all sects and denominations of Irishmen.

The people when thus collected will feel their own weight and secure that power which theory has already admitted as their portion, and to which if they be not aroused by their present provocations to vindicate it, they deserve to forfeit their pretensions for ever.

James Napper Tandy

Not a whisper about violence or revolution throughout the entire proceedings. All they wanted was reform, the abolition of bigotry in religion and politics and the equal distribution of voting and other rights, throughout all sects and denominations of Irishmen.

Despite the great revolutionary forces surging fiercely in other parts of the world, 'reform' was far from the mind of the administration in Ireland at that time and the United Irishmen were soon to learn that corruption was so ingrained in the system that reform was impossible.

The King is Absolute

The Government of Ireland in 1791 consisted of the King, represented by the Viceroy (always an Englishman), the

Lords and the Commons. Everything they decided was subject to overall control by the British Government. The Chief
Secretary and the Lord Chancellor were both appointees of
the British cabinet. The Lords and Commons were composed mainly of bought placemen and pensioners who were
used steadily to outvote the unbought minority.

According to Lecky:

> There were no less than 110 members of the House of Com-
> mons enjoying places and pensions and while the public rev-
> enue of Ireland amounted to £1,600,000 a year, very near one-
> eighth part of this sum was divided among members of Parlia-
> ment ... Almost every piece of lucrative patronage in the coun-
> try was bestowed on members of Parliament or on their rela-
> tions. Peerages were created with a lavishness unknown in
> England, and they were created mainly with the object of pur-
> chasing seats in the House of Commons. The religious denomi-
> nation which comprised at least three-fourths of the people
> was totally unrepresented. Not more than eighty-two seats out
> of the three hundred in the House of Commons were returned
> by counties or considerable towns. Two-thirds of the repre-
> sentatives in that House were returned by less than one hun-
> dred persons ... Between 1585 and 1692 there had been inter-
> vals amounting altogether to nearly eighty-five years during
> which no Irish Parliament sat. During nearly two-thirds of the
> eighteenth century the members of the House of Commons
> held their seats for the entire reign. The House of Lords was so
> constituted that it did not possess even a semblance of inde-
> pendence. At one time the bishops, who were appointed di-
> rectly by the Crown, formed a majority of its active members.
> At other times the constant stream of ministerial partisans that
> was poured into it had made all real opposition an impos-
> sibility. 'By this trade of Parliament,' said Grattan 'the King is
> absolute. His will is signified by both Houses of Parliament,
> who are now as much an instrument in his hand as a bayonet
> in the hands of a regiment. Like a regiment, they have their ad-
> jutant, who goes to the infirmary for the old, and to the brothel
> for the young; and men thus carted as it were into the House
> to vote for the Minister are called the representatives of the
> people.

The peaceful agitation for the reform of this bastion of
corruption went on for the next two and a half years until

the Society of United Irishmen was finally driven underground in May 1794. Seven weeks after its foundation, the
Dublin branch issued a circular letter to their friends all over
the country asking them to organise branches in their own
areas. In this letter, they stated:

> The object of this institution is to make a United Society of the
> Irish nation; to make all Irishmen Citizens – all Citizens Irish-
> men ... We think that whoever desires an amended constitu-
> tion, without including the great body of the people, must on
> his own principles be convicted of political persecution and
> political monopoly ... A more unjust and absurd constitution
> cannot be devised, than that which condemns the natives of a
> country to perpetual servitude, under the arbitrary dominion
> of strangers and slaves.

Towards the end of the same year (late December 1791), the
British Home Secretary (Henry Dundas) wrote to the Viceroy, Lord Westmoreland. In his letter he expressed the concern of the British Cabinet at the reports reaching them of
the attempts being made to unite members of different religious persuasions in Ireland for what they deemed to be
seditious purposes – namely, reform of Parliament, the abolition of bigotry and the granting of equal voting and other
rights to all. While they did not wish to coerce an unwilling
Dublin Castle, they apparently felt that Irish Catholics
should be allowed 'such advantage as can be given them
without danger to the existing establishments and to the
general interests of the Empire'. They specifically referred to
the penal laws still applicable to the professions, trade,
manufacture, intermarriage, education, carrying of arms,
serving either on grand or petty juries.

After consultation with the Irish Privy Council, Westmoreland sent a letter to Prime Minister Pitt on 18 January
1792 in which he gave his considered views on how Ireland
should be governed and on the current agitation for reform:

> It is the general belief that their increasing power, with their
> disproportion of numbers, must eventually, either by influence
> or more probably by force, give the Catholics the upper hand,
> overturn the Church Establishment first, next proceed to the

possession of the State, and the property which had been obtained through conquest ... That the Irish frame of Government like every human institution, has faults is true, but con-
ceiving the object of you and I to be, and which is only our
duty to look to [sic], how England can govern Ireland, that is
how England can govern a country containing one-half as
many inhabitants as herself, and in many respects more advan-
tageously situated, I hold the task not to be easy, but that the
present frame of Irish government is particularly well calculated for our purpose. That frame is a Protestant garrison in
possession of the land, magistracy, and power of the country;
holding that property under the tenure of British power and
supremacy, and ready at every instant to crush the rising of
the conquered ... Do you conceive England can govern Ireland
by the popularity of the Government? ... Is not the very es-
sence of your Imperial policy to prevent the interest of Ireland
clashing and interfering with the interest of England? ... Reflect what Ireland would be in opposition to England, and you
will see the necessity of some very strong interior power or
management that will render Ireland subservient to the general orders of the Empire ... Do you employ a soldier on her account she does not pay, or a single ship more for the protection
of British commerce than if she was at the bottom of the sea? If
she were there it might be one thing but while she exists you
must rule her. Count what she would be in opposition. Have
you not crushed her at every point that would interfere with
British interest or monopoly by means of her Parliament for
the last century, till lately? If, as her Government became more
open and more attentive to the feelings of the Irish nation, the
difficulty of Irish management has increased, is that a reason
for opening the Government and making the Parliament more
subservient to the feelings of the nation at large? ... the risk
ought not to be run in courting them [the Catholics], of over-
setting the attachment of the Protestant power by which England ever has, and whilst that power is prevalent always may
govern Ireland ... The Catholics may at times be useful to
frighten the aristocracy, but in my honest opinion they are an
engine too dangerous for speculation ... It is hardly necessary I
should add that the attempt of the franchise and the abolition
of distinctions is impracticable, and ruinous in the attempt.

The Protestant Ascendancy

In the Viceroy's view, reform of Parliament or the granting
of concessions to Catholics such as the right to vote, carry

arms, or serve on grand juries was out of the question. The Protestant Ascendancy would not wear it and England had no other option but to go along with the Protestant Ascendancy because it was through it alone that the English interest in Ireland could be protected and preserved. He was strongly supported by his Chief Secretary, Hobart, who wrote to the British Home Secretary at the same time:

> The connection between England and Ireland rests absolutely upon the Protestant ascendancy. Abolish distinctions, and you create a Catholic superiority. If you are to maintain a Protestant ascendancy, it must be by substituting influence for numbers ... Whilst you maintain the Protestant ascendancy, the ruling powers in Ireland look to England as the foundation of their authority and influence. The Executive Government of both countries must ever (as it has always been) be under the same control.

The Protestant Parliament in Dublin must, therefore, be allowed to continue unreformed so long as it was able to hold down the Irish people and facilitate the ruling of Ireland in England's interest.

Constitutional Agitation 'Revs Up'

The reaction of the United Irishmen was simply to intensify their agitation for reform. On 14 December 1792, the Dublin branch issued an address of encouragement to the waning Volunteer organisation after the style of Paine and Jefferson and the French:

> Citizen Soldiers! Citizen Soldiers, to arms! Take up the shield of freedom and the pledge of peace ... Every man should become a soldier in the defence of his rights. Liberty is the exercise of all our rights, natural and political, secured to us and our posterity by a real representation of the people; and equality is the extension of the constituent to the fullest dimensions of the constitution of the elective franchise to the whole body of the people....
>   In four words lies all our power – Universal Emancipation and Representative Legislature: yet we are confident that on the pivot of this principle, a convention – still less, a society,

still less, a single man, would be able, first to move, and then to raise the world. We therefore wish for Catholic emancipation without any modification; but still we consider this necessary enfranchisement as merely the portal to the temple of national freedom. Wide as this entrance is – wide enough to admit three millions – it is narrow when compared to the capacity and comprehension of our beloved principle, which takes in every individual of the Irish nation, casts an equal eye over the whole island, embraces all that think, and feels for all that suffer ... In the sincerity of our souls do we desire Catholic emancipation; but were it obtained tomorrow, tomorrow would we go on, as we do today, in the pursuit of that reform which would still be wanting to ratify their liberties as well as our own....

Fourteen long years have elapsed since the rise of your association and in 1782 did you imagine that in 1792 this nation would still remain unrepresented? How many nations in the interval have gotten the start of Ireland? How many of our countrymen have sunken into the grave?

On 15 December 1792, *The Northern Star* published a report of a meeting held by a society called 'The Irish Jacobins of Belfast' declaring *inter alia*:

That this Kingdom has no National Parliament, in as much as the Great Mass of the People are not represented in Parliament. That the People of Ireland, of every Religious Description have an inherent and indefeasible right from God and nature, to constitute Laws for their internal and external Welfare that the People of Ireland can never effectually constitute their own Laws without an extension of the Elective Franchise to all its Citizens. That the Elective Franchise can never be obtained without a cordial, steady, and persevering union of all the Irish People of every denomination....

Less than a fortnight later (26 December 1792), the Belfast Branch of the United Irishmen declared that any nation in which three-quarters of the people were excluded from the legislature, the great majority of what were called its representatives were appointed arbitrarily for a long term of years, taxes without end were levied off the people, and the nation was involved in debt to purchase votes to impose more taxes ... such a nation was a nation of slaves.

On 3 March 1793, the Dublin branch of the Society issued an address to the People of Ireland in which they reiterated their support for full and complete emancipation of the Catholics, repeated their condemnation of intolerance, bigotry and persecution and drew attention to the fact that the Volunteers had been insulted, their artillery had been seized; soldiers were seen hourly with a police magistrate at their head parading the streets, entering and searching the houses of citizens for arms; and finally the officers of the only society which had spirit to observe on these proceedings, were being seized and thrown into prison.

Military Intimidation

All this was too much for the Government. The imperialist's answer to argument and democratic wish is never conciliation or concession, always force, intimidation and the creation of division among the people. A troop of light dragoons was dispatched to Belfast early in January 1793 to arrest the printer and proprietors of *The Northern Star* and convey them to Dublin to stand trial on a charge of seditious libel. On the afternoon of 9 March, four troops of dragoons were sent rampaging through the centre of the city to intimidate the Volunteers and the townspeople. The troops were organised in parties of ten or twenty, each under the command of a corporal or sergeant, and galloped through the central streets at full speed, with sabres drawn, as if charging an enemy, attacking men, women and children and wounding many. On Monday, 11 March 1793, the Viceroy issued a proclamation forbidding all future assemblies of armed men in Belfast or its neighbourhood, and charging the magistrates to disperse all such assemblies of Volunteers. In Parliament a new Militia Act was passed to provide for 16,000 men – 500 in each county who would be available to crush any popular movement. An Arms Act was passed in February 'to prevent the importation of arms, gunpowder, and ammunition into this Kingdom, and the removing and keeping of gunpowder, arms, and ammunition without Licence'.

Both measures were aimed at bringing the increasingly un-
reliable Volunteers under tighter control.

Pitt's Underlying Policy

Against this display of force a Catholic Relief Bill was introduced in April 1793, despite opposition from the Lord Chancellor, John Fitzgibbon, to meet partially the request submit-
ted by the Catholic gentry in their abject petition to His Majesty three months previously. The object of the Bill was to
bribe Catholics into a position whereby they could more
easily be detached from the Protestant reformers in the the
United Irishmen, and to predispose them to look favourably
on the legislative union between Great Britain and Ireland
which, even at this early stage, was actively germinating in
the dark and deep recesses of Pitt's Imperial mind. To prevent at all costs the union between the sects, which the United Irishmen were trying to forge, was the chief aim of English policy in Ireland. Such a union would be against the
English interest. The Act enabled Catholics to vote for Protestant members of Parliament and none other, and they
were also granted some minor rights subject to a humiliating
oath. They were, however, still excluded from the Houses of
Parliament, from the privy council, from the shrievalty and
from almost all judicial and Government positions.

However, Black Jack (John Fitzgibbon) was not to be
outdone. His busy brain was already maturing a series of
measures to deprive all Irishmen – particularly the United
Irishmen – of expressing their wishes by delegates, and
every means of asserting their rights by arms. Chief of these
was the Convention Bill introduced by himself in the Lords
in April 1793, forbidding the summoning of any delegated
or representative assembly except Parliament, on the pretext
that such assemblies may be used 'to serve the ends of fac-
tious and seditious persons, to the violation of the public
peace, and the great and manifest encouragement of riot,
tumult and disorder'. The immediate object of the measure
was to prevent a convention of the United Irishmen in

Athlone for which the writs had already been issued. It became law in July 1793 and remained in force until 1879. Throughout these eight score and six years it was used repeatedly to muzzle freedom of expression and to prevent the people of Ireland from freely discussing their affairs in public. In the words of John Mitchell: 'It was the rock ahead which confronted O'Connell in all his agitation. This law it was which prevented his calling together the promised "Council of Three Hundred" and left only the alternative of inorganic "Monster meetings" – which latter indeed were also made criminal by a prudent interpretation of the law'.

Spies and Informers

From its inception, the Society of United Irishmen was riddled with spies and informers. All were well rewarded for their information. Through such channels, the Government was always well informed about what was going on – who was in the organisation, who attended meetings, took the test and became members, who appeared to be the more dangerous radicals and who were no more than left-wing agitators. All this information was very useful and was generally accurate. When the time came to pounce, the Government knew whom to strike and where to find them.

In the spring of 1794, a certain Anglican clergyman named Jackson appeared in Dublin on a mission from France. He wanted to make contact with the United Irishmen. He was accompanied by an old friend, an English barrister named Cockayne, whom he picked up en route, in London. Cockayne was now working as a British spy. 'From this moment,' wrote Tone's son long afterwards, 'the life of Jackson was completely in the power of the British Government. His evil genius was already pinned upon him; his mission from France, his every thought, and his views, were known. He was allowed to proceed not in order to detect an existing conspiracy in Ireland but to form one, and thus increase the number of victims'. He soon succeeded in meeting Hamilton Rowan who was then in Newgate prison awaiting trial.

Through Rowan he met Tone who wrote a statement for him about conditions in Ireland which in due course fell into the hands of the British via Cockayne. On 29 April 1794, he was arrested and charged with treason but was not brought to trial until a year later when, presumably, he was deemed to be of no further use. On 1 May 1794, Rowan escaped from prison and made his way to America via France just in time to save his own skin. For reasons best known to the 'Administration', Tone was left alone. He was destined for some other role which not even God nor Mr Pitt had determined at this stage. In May 1795, Tone went to America via Belfast along with his wife and family. From there he went on to France leaving his wife and family behind in America. By 1 April 1796 he had arrived in France where he spent the rest of his life, until after the Rebellion of 1798, negotiating with the French Government for military aid for Ireland.

End of Constitutional Agitation

Four days after Rowan's escape, the King's Storm Troopers smashed their way into the meeting place of the United Irishmen at Tailor's Hall in Back Lane, dispersed the members and seized the papers of the Society. More than three million of the common people were at this time without representation in Parliament and had no more say in the management of their own affairs than the Negroes in America. Under the Convention Act, they were deprived of the right to assemble and consult with one another about their problems. Trial by Jury was virtually abolished and no man's life or liberty had any longer the slightest protection under the law. The Society was thus driven underground and, as happens when people's natural right to liberty is being denied and cannot be secured by democratic means, the people took steps to secure such right by the only other means open to them – namely, armed conspiracy and physical force. The re-organisation of the Society upon revolutionary and military lines began late in 1794, three years after its foundation, when all attempts to secure its objectives by constitutional agitation had been tried and found wanting.

PART 2: The Slaves Revolt

Following the partial war-time coalition in England between Pitt's party and the opposition, it was agreed in August 1794 that Lord Fitzwilliam would replace Westmoreland as Viceroy in Dublin. Fitzwilliam's policy was to give the three million Catholics in Ireland the same voting rights as Protestants and to reform the corrupt Castle administration. Pitt did not agree with this policy but he knew that Fitzwilliam would not accept the post without his (Pitt's) tacit approval. Pitt's policy was to subvert the budding union between the different sects in Ireland at all costs, provoke an armed insurrection which would enable him to crush the United Irishmen and prepare the way for enforced legislative union of Great Britain and Ireland. On arrival in Dublin in January 1795, one of Fitzwilliam's first acts by way of cleaning up the corrupt administration was to remove John Beresford from the not very prominent office of Commissioner of the Revenue.

John Beresford – King of Ireland

Descended from one Tristram Beresford who came to Ireland during the reign of James I as manager of the London Company of Planters, John Beresford had succeeded in establishing himself as one of the leading figures in the Castle administration. According to Lecky:

> He was one of the most distinguished examples of a class of politicians who were a peculiar and characteristic product of the Irish political system. He belonged to a family which, though entirely undistinguished in Parliament and in responsible statesmanship, had secured so large a proportion of the minor offices in administration, had employed its patronage so exclusively for the purpose of building up a family influence, and had formed in this manner so extensive a system of political connections and alliances, that it had become one of the most powerful controlling and directing influences in the Government of Ireland.

Quoting from a paper drawn up in 1791, he continues:

'... the party which was called the Beresford party is reckoned at only eight members, but it is added that the Chancellor, the Attorney-General, and Cooke were allied with it. John Beresford, was the First Commissioner, with an official house and a salary of £2,000 a year, and he had obtained the office of Taster of Wines, with a salary of £1,000 a year, for his own life and that of his eldest son. His son Marcus – an active and useful member of the House – was first counsel to the commissioner with a salary of £2,000. His second son, John Claudius had a very lucrative office in the revenue. His son-in-law would probably be provided for in the first law arrangement.' His brother was the first Marquis of Waterford. Another brother, William, was Protestant Bishop of Ossory. He (William) looked for the highest Church preferment, and he was married to the Chancellor's sister. The son of the Bishop was member for the episcopal borough. The Chancellor had a large following, and the Attorney General sat in the House of Commons with his son and his nephew. Lord Waterford had the patronage of the counties of Waterford and Derry. 'This party,' it was added, 'undoubtedly govern the kingdom ... Lord Waterford is said to stand remarkably well with the King, and to have had a constant connection with England with the persons who had the ear of the minister, such as Mr Robinson, Mr Rose, etc.'

There was apparently no stop to the rise of Beresford's influence. Lecky comments:

A few years after the vice-royalty of Lord Fitzwilliam, it was said that at least a fourth of all the places in the island were filled with dependents or connections of the Beresfords, and during Fitzwilliam's time the influence of John Beresford was, or was believed to be, so overwhelming, that he was called the King of Ireland. He was politically closely allied with the Chancellor, who was bitterly and notoriously hostile to Fitzwilliam and his policy ... He was strenuously opposed to the Catholic policy of the Viceroy....

Fitzwilliam insisted that 'his confidential servants should be men in whom he could confide; ... that family cabals for monopolising the power of the state should be broken up; and that the Government, and Government patronage, in all its branches, should be in the hands of the representative of the Sovereign'. Though he removed Beresford from office, he granted him his entire official salary for life, and gave him an assurance that none of the other members of his family would be removed. 'They were still left,' said Fitzwilliam, 'in the full enjoyment of more emoluments than ever were accumulated in any country upon one family'. This was two hundred years before Saddam Hussein and Nicolae Ceauçescu learned how to set up their own families and feather their nests at the expense of the common people.

The Viceroy was soon to discover who was the real boss in Dublin. Beresford went immediately after his dismissal to England. He met the King and he met Prime Minister Pitt. Fitzwilliam met his Waterloo and on 25 March 1795 he left Dublin, eleven weeks and four days after his arrival there, to commence what he intended to be a liberal term of office. But that was not to be. 'A certain family cabal,' wrote Burke 'were in the sole possession of the ear of the Government'. Five days later the new Viceroy, Lord Camden, arrived amidst such public hostility, that the military had to be called out to suppress the popular disturbance in the streets. In the words of Mitchell, the arrival of this gentleman, 'gave the signal for the bloody anarchy through which Ireland was doomed to pass for the next four years, and which, it was deliberately calculated, was to end in her extinction as a nation'.

The Union – An Imperial Necessity

No more was to be done about granting equality of voting rights to the three million helots in Ireland. Instead, a repressive military régime was to be put in train, aimed at crushing the organisation which was preaching unity among the sects in the cause of democracy and which the British regarded as inimical to their interest. Pitt believed that a passive and subject Ireland could only be brought about by a legislative union between the two countries, and he strongly believed also, under the continued guidance of his most trustworthy adviser on Irish affairs – Chancellor John Fitzgibbon – that in order to pave the way for such a union it was necessary to provoke an insurrection, which would frighten sufficient of the loyalist garrison into compliance with his aims and simultaneously enable him to attack and destroy the United Irishmen. If the disabilities from which the people were suffering were remedied, there would be no insurrection and then there would be no union. Accordingly, the people had to be left with their disabilities, and at the same time goaded into revolt by a campaign of severe military oppression. Nothing else could explain the campaign of torture and murder of unarmed civilians – men, women and children – conducted by the British army in Ireland from 1795 until the enforced annexation of the country by Britain under the Act of Union 1800.

Castle Propaganda

The Castle authorities lost no time in putting the policy of provocation and terrorisation into effect. Almost immediately, Government agents were sent to Armagh to curb the growth of the United Irishmen by stirring up the agrarian discord which existed in that county between the Peep-o-Day Boys (Protestants) and the Defenders (Catholics) into a religious conflict, on the specious grounds of zeal for Church and King. Groundless rumours were invented and circulated, about intended massacres of all the Protestant people by the Catholics. 'Efforts were made,' wrote Dr Madden, 'to infuse into the mind of the Protestant, feelings of distrust in his Catholic fellow-countrymen. "Popish plots and conspiracies" were fabricated with a practical facility, which some influential authorities conceived it no degradation to stoop to, and alarming reports of these dark confederations were circulated with a restless assiduity'.

As intended, this malicious propaganda had the effect of rousing the fears and hatreds of the Peep-o-Day Boys who were much in the majority in the area and also had an abundance of arms. They took vigorous action to expel their neighbours. Notices were posted on the cabins of Catholic tenants ordering them to 'Hell or Connaught' by a certain date, and if they didn't comply they were burnt out. Many

murders were committed. It is estimated that some 7,000
persons in all were either killed or burnt out in that small
area alone at that particular time. The discord culminated, in
September 1795, in a skirmish between the sects, known as
the 'Battle of the Diamond', which ended with the foundation of the Orange Order. Pitt's policy of keeping the sects at
one another's throats was working well. The Commander-
in-Chief of His Majesty's forces, Lord Carhampton, had
troops conveniently deployed around Armagh to pick up
any young men of military age who might be found wan-
dering about after their parents' cabins had been burnt
down; initially for transfer to one of the 'tenders' also conveniently anchored in various sea-ports around the coast;
and subsequently for posting to His Majesty's men-of-war.
This was what Carhampton described as 'vigour beyond the
law' – a delicate phrase used widely by him and other members of the administration to describe outrages committed by
magistrates against the law.

Commenting on the situation in that first year of intensified oppression – namely, 1795 – Mitchell wrote: 'During
all the rest of this year the greater part of Leinster, with portions of Ulster and Munster, were in the utmost terror and
agony; the Orange magistrates, aided by the troops, arrest-
ing and imprisoning, without any charge, multitudes of un-
offending people, under one pretext or another'.

Meanwhile the re-organisation of the United Irishmen
into an oath-bound military body under county and provincial commanders, a central Directory and Commander-in-
Chief had been proceeding apace. It appears that Ulster had
been organised by May 1795 and that the organisation of
Leinster had begun in the autumn of the following year.

'Stripped naked of law and of government'

Early in 1796 the new Viceroy had enacted a further series of
repressive measures, in addition to the bottomless armoury
already in existence, designed to hasten insurrection. An
Insurrection Act gave magistrates almost unlimited powers

to arrest and imprison, and search houses for arms. It also provided that the administering of unlawful oaths was a felony punishable by death. It alleged that this provision was necessary to combat Defenderism and Orangeism although nobody was ever charged with administering the Orange oath to exterminate Catholics. In fact, the provision was not directed specifically against either the Defenders or the Orangemen but against the United Irishmen, the only association of whose doctrines the Government had the slightest fear. An important clause in the Act empowered any two magistrates to seize persons who should publish or sell a newspaper or pamphlet which they, the two magistrates, should deem seditious, and without any form of trial send them on board the fleet. This amounted to total suppression of all press save the Castle press. Another clause enabled the magistrates to take up idle vagrants and persons who had no visible means of living, and send them on board the fleet. An Indemnity Act indemnified magistrates and military officers, who might have acted against the forms and rules of law or exceeded the ordinary forms and rules of law, against the consequences of their illegal actions. It gave the powers of martial law without the necessity of proclaiming it, and was an actual invitation to break the law.

Grattan maintained that 'offending magistrates were thus protected against the consequences of their outrages and their illegalities ... that the poor were stricken out of the protection of the law, and the rich out of its penalties ... that because of the Government inspired rumours of intended Popish uprisings, magistrates conceived that the law now made it a merit to break the law, provided it were done in the oppression and ruin of the Catholic people ... and that they felt that they were turned loose with a full commission to burn, slay, rob, and ravish'. Only one thing more was needed to gain absolute control over the bodies and souls of nine-tenths of the people – the suspension of the Habeas Corpus Act. This was obtained on 13 October 1796, and in the words of Mitchell, 'From that moment Ireland stood stripped naked of all law and government'.

'The French are in the Bay'

On 21 December 1796, a substantial French expeditionary
force, with Wolfe Tone aboard, stood at the entrance to Bantry Bay waiting to put ashore. Through its wide network of
spies, plants, stooges and special messengers, the British
Government had full and accurate information about this
expedition. The proposed point of invasion was deemed by
Tone to be inadvisable. He favoured a landing on the east
coast somewhere near Dublin or Belfast. In the month of
October or November, a special messenger was dispatched
from France, informing the Irish Directory that the expedition which had been under discussion for some months
would consist of 14,000 troops together with a quantity of
arms and ammunition sufficient to equip up to 45,000 rebels.
The British, however, were at the same time in a position to
deceive the leaders of the United Irishmen with false information. A few days after the departure of the first messenger, it appears that a further letter from France was received
from the Irish Directory, which was considered by them as
authentic, stating that the proposed expedition was postponed for some months.

This second letter was obviously a fabrication and
would explain why no steps were taken to organise the
United Irishmen in West Cork to receive the French. Outside
the cities and big urban areas where copies of the *Freeman's
Journal* and other papers could be had, not many people
knew what was going on in the world at large at this time.
Few had heard of the French Republic, or of the United Irish
Society, or of liberty, equality, and fraternity. Indeed, the
poor people around Beara and Bantry were so ignorant and
ill-prepared that they regarded the French expeditionary
force as a hostile invasion. Plowden states that when a boat
went ashore from the squadron to reconnoitre the country,
'it was immediately captured, and multitudes appeared on
the beach in readiness to oppose a landing'. A similar thing
happened in Mayo two years later. When the French landed
at Killala in 1798 it is recorded that the people were afraid
and gathered around them at the Fair Green at Lahardane,

not understanding their language or why they had come.

Except in places where the United Irish military system, however limited, was in place, the people were not, as Tone correctly advised, able to take advantage of the foreign help being offered to them. The British were undoubtedly aware of this also, which would explain why they took no steps to oppose the Bantry landing. They knew as well the inherent difficulties – a wild coast, surrounded by desolate mountains, where there were but small resources for a commissariat, where no good horses could be found for the artillery and wagons and where, above all else, no insurrection was likely, because there were no United Irishmen organised in the area.

In effect, nothing was accomplished by the expedition. Many of the ships were scattered and lost as a result of bad weather, and no landing could be made. The remnants of the fleet arrived back in Brest on 1 January 1797, sixteen days after it set sail on 15 December. Significantly, not a single British ship was sighted during the entire operation.

Official Policy of Murder and Terrorism

Much has been written about the atrocities committed against the common people of Ireland, almost entirely Catholics, by the British army, by the magistrates and by Orangemen during Lord Camden's Viceroyalty, particularly from 1796 to 1798. While there is no doubt that numerous acts of torture, brutality and murder were committed by these bodies during the period in question, it must nevertheless be remembered that all such crimes were committed pursuant to an official policy of provocation approved at the highest level. Nobody was ever brought to trial for such offences and the perpetrators were fully indemnified against any breaches of the law which they may have committed. In the final analysis, ultimate responsibility for all such murders and terrorist actions must rest with King George III and Prime Minister Pitt who laid down the policy, and with the

senior military and political commanders who directed and
controlled its execution.

'Vigour Beyond the Law'

Commenting on the events of the time in a pamphlet published in London in 1797 under the signature of 'an Observ-
er', the author, who happened to be a Justice of the Peace in
one of the northern counties, says:

> Shortly after peace was concluded with America, the minister
> perceived they had been playing a losing game in Ireland; the
> Volunteer association had materially altered the face of the
> country; in many places the Catholics had embodied them-
> selves into a Volunteer corps; a friendly intercourse with their
> Protestant brethren naturally followed; they felt that as Irish-
> men their interests were co-equal, hatred on account of reli-
> gion was banished, harmony prevailed, and, if not an union of
> affection, at least an union of political sentiment appeared to
> exist amongst the people; of this, administration was well in-
> formed, and ministers trembled for what might be the result.
> To avert 'reformation' they felt it 'their duty' to create 'divi-
> sion'. Various were the means employed to effect this immoral
> object among others, they reverted to the old diabolical one of
> fomenting those religious feuds, which had so often consum-
> ed the vitals and palsied the native energy of the land.
>
> They taught the weak and credulous Protestant and Pres-
> byterian to believe that, if the Catholics who had obtained
> arms during the war were suffered to retain them, they would
> seize on the first opportunity to overturn the Government, and
> erect Popery on the ruins of the Protestant religion. This, and
> other acts equally insidious, had the desired effect on the
> minds of many persons, particularly in the county of Ar-
> magh....
>
> Here fanaticism reared her standard, and a number of
> deluded people entered into a combination for the purpose of
> depriving the Catholics of their arms by force.
>
> For some time the Catholics remained patient...; at length
> they declared that all their efforts to obtain legal redress had
> been unavailing, and that the necessity of the case would
> oblige them to enter into counter-combinations to defend their
> lives and properties against a banditti of plundering ruffians,
> who appeared to be countenanced by authority, inasmuch as
> they were not punished by the criminal law of the land. These
> two parties had several encounters, in which victory was

various; but many of the Catholic party wearied out by continual persecution, fled from Armagh to different parts of the kingdom, particularly to the counties of Louth and Meath.

Led by passion and goaded by persecution, they proceeded (like the Peep-of-Day Boys, who first set the example, and who never were punished) to acts of felony, by taking arms by force; ... This then ... was the true origin and progress of Defenderism in Ireland.

He gave details of specific outrages:

In county Meath, a party of Defenders who had taken shelter from an army attack at length offered to surrender, but when the army entered the building they put every Defender to death. The body of each man, 'killed off' was cast from a window into the street, and for this ... the soldiers were not even reprimanded.

In county Louth a party was attacked by a squadron of dragoons – those who escaped the sword were driven into a river and drowned.

In county Cavan a party of Defenders took refuge from an army attack in the village of Ballanaugh ... The magistrates and officers commanding ordered the soldiers to surround and set fire to the village which order was readily obeyed ... Many innocent people perished in the flames with the guilty.

In the counties of Westmeath, Longford, and Monaghan, similar excesses were committed.

The administration was afraid to let the atrocities which had been committed meet the public eye and ministers procured a bill of indemnity to be passed in parliament to screen from punishment those officers of the 'peace' who at the hour of midnight, tore men from the arms of their families, merely on the suspicion of their being 'seditious'....

In January 1796, a party of Orangemen, the Peep-of–Day Boys, headed by William Trimble, attacked and robbed Daniel Corrigan a reputable citizen (a dealer in cattle) in the parish of Kilmore county of Armagh ... Twenty minutes later Tremble returned and murdered Mr Corrigan by lodging seven balls in his body. Tremble was tried and found guilty but through a 'certain' interference was respited and 'suffered' to go on board the fleet like 'a good and loyal subject'.

The above is only a fraction of the list of outrages. A few of the other terrorist acts perpetrated by the military during the reign of terror introduced in Ulster by General Lake in 1797 are also worth a mention.

An organ which supported United Irishmen opinion, namely the *Morning Star*, was ordered to publish an article reflecting on the loyalty of the people of Belfast. When the article did not appear, a detachment of soldiers marched into the printing offices next morning and demolished them, breaking the presses, scattering the types and seizing the books. It never rose again. Neilson, the first editor, and the two Simms, the proprietors, had already been lodged in Newgate without being charged. At the same time the chief Government paper of the day, the *Faulkner's Journal*, an organ obviously in the pay of the Castle, was publishing savage denunciations of Catholics, Defenders and United Irishmen, but only praise for the Armagh Orangemen.

Under powers conferred by the proclamation issued on 17 May 1797, Lord Carhampton, the Commander-in-Chief, without waiting for orders from civil magistrates, ordered the military to act in dispersing tumultuous or unlawful assemblies. Henceforth, it was left to the discretion of the military to determine what was an unlawful assembly; and that often included families asleep in their own beds, if it was suspected that they had weapons in the house, or that a United Irish oath had ever been administered there.

On 14 October 1797, William Orr, a respectable Presbyterian was hanged at Carrickfergus having, on the evidence of a witness who admitted subsequently that he had sworn falsely, been found guilty of administering the United Irish oath. The conviction was appealed to the Viceroy, on the grounds of perjury and the fact that some members of the jury were drunk, but without effect.

In spite of repression, the United Irishmen organisation continued to grow in Leinster and to a lesser extent in parts of Munster. Pitt was concerned because it had not appeared as an organised army that could be engaged and destroyed. In his opinion, more decisive measures were required to incite an insurrection. Carhampton disagreed with the policy and resigned. He wanted to suppress the existing secret organisation rather than incite a rebellion. He was succeeded by General Abercrombie who, after a tour of the country, found the army in such a state of indiscipline as a result of the crimes committed by them against the people, that he also resigned. 'Within these twelve months,' he wrote, 'every crime, every cruelty that could be committed by Cossacks or Calmucks, has been transacted here ... I have found the cavalry in general unfit for service, and more than one-half of the infantry dispersed over the face of the country, in general under officers very little able to command them. At Fermoy more than three-fourths of the light infantry are "on command"'. On 26 February 1798, he issued his famous General Order deploring that, 'The very disgraceful frequency of courts-martial, and the many complaints of the conduct of the troops in this kingdom ... proved the army to be in a state of licentiousness, which must render it formidable to every one but the enemy'.

According to Sir Jonah Barrington, 'Pitt counted on the expertness of the Irish Government to effect a premature explosion. Free quarters were now ordered, to irritate the Irish population; slow tortures were inflicted under the pretence of forcing confessions; the people were goaded and driven to madness'.

After Abercrombie's resignation, General Lake took over command of the armed forces, and Chief Secretary Pelham was replaced by the infamous Lord Castlereagh. The way was now set for the implementation of the bloody conspiracy upon which Pitt had embarked. He had concentrated in Ireland a force of at least 130,000 men including regular troops, English and Scottish fencible regiments and Irish militia. On 30 March, the whole country was put under martial law by proclamation. 'From that moment on,' said Myles Byrne, 'everyone considered himself walking on a mine, ready to be blown up'. On 23 April, two regiments of 'foreign troops' had been ordered into Ireland – the Hessians, German mercenaries from Hesse Darmstadt and Hesse Cassel. Troops were billeted in 'free quarters' amongst the ordinary families of the countryside, and orders were issued from the Castle that the military should in their absolute discretion take all measures which they should consider necessary for suppressing the rebellion which did not yet exist but which, it was determined, should immediately break out. Hanging until half-dead, picketing, and driving suspects mad with caps of lighting pitch fixed to their hair became the order of the day. The magistrates of the 'Ascendancy' were at the same time assured that whatever they should think fit to do against the people would be condoned.

According to Byrne:

> Many of the low-bred magistrates availed themselves of the martial law to torture inoffensive country people. Archibald Hamilton Jacob and the Enniscorthy Yeomen Cavalry never marched out of the town without being accompanied by a regular executioner, with his ropes, cat-o'-nine-tails etc. Hawtry White, Solomon Richards, and a Protestant minister of the name of Owens, were all notorious for their cruelty and persecuting spirit; the latter particularly so, putting on pitch caps and exercising other torments ... Although several of the principal chiefs of the United Irishmen were Protestants, the Orange magistrates did all they could to spread the belief that the Catholics had no other object in view but to kill their Protestant fellow-subjects, and to give weight to this opinion, they did what they could to provoke the unfortunate people to commit outrages and reprisals, by killing some and burning their houses. The infamous Hunter Gowan raised a cavalry corps comprising about thirty or forty low Orangemen which went by the name of the Black Mob ... They arrested all the Catholic blacksmiths, and burnt their houses ... Garrett Fennell who had just landed from England ... was met by this corps, and tied by his two hands up to a tree; they then stood at a certain distance and each man lodged the contents of his carbine in the body of poor Fennell, at their Captain's command ... Fennell left a young widow and two children. In a house close by they wantonly murdered the occupant, James Darcy, father of five children. The day after this event, 25 May 1798, twenty-eight fathers of families, prisoners, were massacred in the Ball Alley of Carnew, without trial. Mr Cope the Protestant minister, was one of the principal magistrates who presided at this execution ... At Dunlavin, previous to the rising, thirty-four men were shot without any trial....

It was an essential element in Pitt's plans for the provocation of insurrection to turn Orange Societies against their

Catholic neighbours. Grattan declared that 'the Ministry was in league with the abettors of the Orange Boys, and at war with the people'. Giving evidence before the Secret Committee after the rebellion, Arthur O'Connor said, 'As one of the executive, it came to my knowledge that considerable sums of money were expended throughout the nation in endeavouring to extend the Orange system, and that the oath of extermination was administered'. The extermination of thousands of people in County Armagh alone is well authenticated, and the conduct of the Orange yeomanry in Leinster in 1798 was notorious.

The People Fight Back

The protracted goading of the people eventually produced a largely unorganised popular explosion which lasted little more than a month from 23 May until the end of June 1798. The outburst turned out to be much more than a rebellion of United Irishmen alone. The many thousands who took to the field included, as well as sworn United Irishmen, large numbers of Defenders and country people who belonged to no organisation but were driven to revolt in self-defence, as well as an unknown number of hangers-on with indifferent motives.

All the leaders of the supreme executive and of the Leinster Directory of the United Irish organisation itself had been arrested immediately prior to the outbreak, with the result that central direction of the revolt by that organisation as originally planned, was totally absent. Local leaders were elected on the spot as the situation developed, and many of them – Fathers John and Michael Murphy, Bagenal Harvey, Edmund Ryan, Kelly of Killann, Byrne, Holt and Dwyer of Wicklow, McCracken, Hope and Munro of Ulster, Matthew Keogh and others – showed themselves to be excellent natural leaders. If they did not achieve results commensurate with their abilities and their efforts it was because of circumstances beyond their control. The rebel force they were called upon to direct was not an army at all, but rapidly

assembled, enthusiastic and unwieldy bodies of indifferently
armed civilians, without military training or organisation, or
adequate supplies. Some were armed with pikes, a small
number had muskets, but a great many had nothing more
than what came readily to hand.

Initial outbreaks were localised, spontaneous and unco-
ordinated and were confined mainly to Co. Wexford and, to
a lesser extent, Antrim and Down. Some minor skirmishes
occurred elsewhere in Ulster and Leinster. Despite their lack
of arms and other deficiencies, the rebels had a number of
initial successes which might have led on to more substantial successes had intelligence and communications been
better. For brief periods they held the principal towns of
Wexford – Gorey, New Ross and Enniscorthy: Wexford
town itself along with most of the county was under their
total control from 30 May until the surrender on 22 June.

Ultimately, lack of fire-power, military training and organisation decided the day against the rebels, and they were
defeated by the superior arms, organisation and training of
regular troops – infantry, cavalry and artillery. Although
militarily a failure – and evidence that ill-armed, untrained
and unorganised men, however valiant, are no match for
well-armed, organised regular forces – 1798, nevertheless,
showed that the common people of the countryside had the
courage to stand up to such an enemy, and that given proper
arms and training in their use, they could, at some future
date, physically force Britain to relinquish control over Ireland, as the colonists had done in America fifteen years
earlier.

PART 3: 'The troops could not be stopped'

Although the immediate cause of rebellion in 1798 was undoubtedly the campaign of murder and terrorism initiated
by the regular troops of the British army and the auxiliary
forces – yeomanry and militia – during the preceding years
of the decade, the more deep-rooted cause which fuelled it,
once it had broken out, was the murder and terrorism perpetrated by Britain over previous centuries, the confiscation
of the land and the near total destruction of the Irish nation.
The visible signs of subjugation were everywhere – arrogant
and rapacious landlords, religious bigotry at every turn, and
a law which had only recently begun to recognise the existence of Irish Roman Catholics.

For seven years the United Irishmen had been advocating amelioration of the lot of the majority. This could be
achieved through reform of the electoral system, elimination
of corruption, and repeal of the repressive laws based on
religious discrimination. The power, property and privilege
established by the confiscations were, however, so well entrenched and protected by the military and legal arms of the
state, and so impervious to change, that the social and
economic conditions of the poor in Ireland in 1798 were little
different from what they had been half a century before,
when Chesterfield described them as worse than those of
Negroes. Despite the social advances being made elsewhere
following revolution in America and France, rack-renting,
tithes, tithe proctors and bailiffs were still, and would remain for many a day yet, part and parcel of everyday life in
Ireland. Accordingly, when the boil burst in May 1798, all
the poison, arising from the denial of man's natural right to
liberty and good usage, poured out, and drove thousands of
totally unorganised people into action along with those who
were already sworn members of the United Irishmen.

With so much wrong on their side, Pitt and Fitzgibbon
rightly feared that if the reforms advocated by the United
Irishmen were implemented, majority rule would follow

and the whole unjust political and economic system built on
the title conferred by successive confiscations would col-
lapse. The main focus of their attack, therefore, was the Society of United Irishmen, the only organised body in existence
which could spearhead a popular revolt against the entrenched ascendancy position. Their strategy was clear –
provoke an insurrection, pounce on the leadership before
anything happened, destroy as much as possible of the organisation in combat, pursue the remnants until all opposition was ended, unite Ireland and Britain by a legislative union and thus reduce Irish nationalism, Protestant and Catholic, to a minority position in the Parliament of the United
Kingdom.

All of Mr Pitt's subsequent actions against the United
Irishmen fit perfectly into this plan:

An insurrection was made inevitable by the campaign of
murder and terrorism conducted by the British military
from 1795. That insurrection broke out on 23 May 1798.

The entire leadership was arrested immediately before the outbreak, which left the organisation leaderless
and out of effective overall control during the rebellion.

Thousands lost their lives in action in the two prov-
inces where the rebellion occurred, namely Leinster and
Ulster.

When the fighting ceased at the end of June, the
hunt for surviving members went on relentlessly. Thousands more were captured, tortured and hanged or sent
aboard the British Fleet.

An Act providing for the annexation of Ireland by
Britain came into effect on 1 January 1801.

Certain commentators often try to represent that the rebellion of 1798 in Wexford degenerated into a religious war in
which the Catholics, led by their priests, forgot about the
most fundamental aim of the United Irishmen – namely to
unite Irishmen of all sects – and brutally murdered their
Protestant neighbours. This is a gross misrepresentation of

the facts. Even Cornwallis, who took up his appointment as Lord Lieutenant on 20 June 1798 when the rebellion was almost over, was shocked at similar comments being made then. 'The violence of our friends,' he said, 'and their folly in endeavouring to make it a religious war, added to the ferocity of our troops, who delight in murder, most powerfully counteract all plans of conciliation ... The minds of people are now in such a state that nothing but blood will satisfy them; and although they will not admit the term, their conversation and conduct point to no other mode of concluding this unhappy business than that of extirpation. ... The conversation even at my table, where you will suppose I do all I can to prevent it, always turns on hanging, shooting, burning etc, etc, and if a priest has been put to death, the greatest joy is expressed by the whole company'.

John Mitchel adds in his *History of Ireland*:

> This was not a 'Popish' rebellion, although every effort was made to give it a sectarian character – first by disarming and disgracing the Catholic yeomanry, next by burning chapels and maltreating priests, and further by the direct incitements and encouragement given to the Orange yeomanry (who were brought into the county for the purpose), to practise their favourite plan of exterminating Catholics. Yet some of the most trusted leaders of the people were Protestants; as Harvey, Grogan, one of the two Colcloughs, Anthony Perry and Keogh Commandant of Wexford. There was, it is true, one Protestant church defaced ... but not till long after several Catholic chapels had been demolished. It may be affirmed that whatever there were of religious rancour in the contest was the work of the Government through its Orange allies, and with the express purpose of preventing an union of Irishmen of all creeds – a thing which is felt to be incompatible with British Government in Ireland.

The incontestable fact of course is, that the war in Wexford was in no way a religious war between Catholics and Protestants, but rather a widespread insurrection of the ordinary people of the countryside (most of whom happened to be Catholics, suffering the gravest economic and political disabilities) against the perpetrators of murders, pitch-capping,

hanging, whipping and every other form of torture, namely
the regular troops of the British army, the yeomanry, militia
and magistrates. It was only when hundreds of Catholic
homes, Catholic chapels and other buildings were burnt
down by armed troops for no reason other than to provoke
terror, that the people naturally crowded around priests like
Fr John Murphy of Boulavogue, Fr Michael Murphy of
Ballycanew and Fr Philip Roche from Gorey, as the only
leaders available to them. In areas where United Irish leaders such as Bagenal Harvey, Matthew Keogh, Perry, Grogan,
Grey and others – all Protestants – came forward to lead, the
people followed them also in their thousands.

Even the much referred to massacre at Scullabogue,
which is repeatedly cited to support the sectarian theory, has
to be considered in the light of all the circumstances of the
day. Scullabogue house was beside the rebel camp at Cor-
bett Hill about a mile from New Ross in which the rebels
had lodged some 200 prisoners, most but not all of whom
were Protestants. New Ross was attacked and captured by
the rebels on the morning of 5 June 1798 but the defender,
General Johnston, counter-attacked and recaptured it in the
afternoon amidst 'shocking carnage' of the rebels. 'The
troops,' according to Major Vesey, 'could not be stopped'.
Rebel losses were estimated at between 2,000 and 3,000 as
against 230 on the loyalist side. It appears that a party of
runaways from the battle had reached Scullabogue declaring
that the rebel army at New Ross had been cut off; that the
troops were shooting all prisoners, and butchering all the
Catholics who fell into their hands (which was true) and that
orders had been issued that all the prisoners at Scullabogue
should be killed (which appears to be untrue). One of the
prisoners in the house on 4 June stated in evidence subsequently that the rebels 'had received intelligence that the
military were again putting all the rebel prisoners to death
in the town of Ross, as they had done at Dunlavin and Carnew'. The leader of the rebel guard is said to have resisted
the order but to have been eventually overwhelmed by the
rabble around him.

The massacre at Scullabogue has all the marks of being the work of a small band of vengeful civilians, acting without authority, but the massacres at New Ross, Dunlavin and Carnew were carried out under the direction and control of organised British military forces. On 24 May, thirty-four prisoners were executed at Dunlavin without trial and on the next day, twenty-eight 'were all taken out of jail and deliberately shot in the Ball Alley at Carnew by the yeomen and a party of Antrim militia in the presence of their officers', before there was any outbreak of rebellion, in these areas. While a certain number of loyalist collaborators and informers were killed during the rebellion and some innocent people also suffered, there is no evidence whatever of a deliberate campaign by the rebels, of murdering Protestants.

The Pitt-bull Grip

By the end of 1798, all but a few of the leaders of the United Irishmen were either killed in action, executed or in prison. The rebellion was over and, although thousands still secretly belonged to it, the Society of United Irishmen was a broken force. The way was clear, therefore, for the creation of the legislative union between Great Britain and Ireland which was the fundamental reason for the bloody anarchy of the previous four years. The Act of annexation which united Ireland and Britain into the United Kingdom of Great Britain and Ireland came into operation with effect from 1 January 1801. Mr Pitt had had his way at last. A rearguard action to undo his grip by military force was launched three years later by the short-lived rebellion of Robert Emmet. Though doomed to failure in the military sense because of disparity of forces, Emmet's rising still occupies an honoured place in the age-long war of attrition against British rule in Ireland.

With the bulk of the commanders now safely disposed of, and the Act of Union securely in place, the main outstanding problem was the disposal of the surviving political leaders. Of these Lecky writes:

The great majority of the more conspicuous United Irishmen at
this period, as well as in the subsequent periods of the movement, were nominally either Presbyterians or members of the
Established Church, though a large proportion of them were
indifferent to theological doctrines. Tone, Butler, Emmet, Hamilton Rowan, Napper Tandy, Arthur O'Connor, Lord Edward
Fitzgerald, Bond, Russell, Drennan, Neilson, and the two
Sheares were all Protestants, and Belfast and other parts of
Presbyterian Ulster were the special centres of Irish republicanism. On this point the Government dispatches and the
writings of the United Irishmen were perfectly agreed.

A number of those listed by Lecky were already dead or out
of the country. Simon Butler died in 1797. Lord Edward
Fitzgerald died on 4 June 1798 from wounds received resist-
ing arrest. He was thirty-five. The two Sheares were hanged
on 14 July 1798. Oliver Bond died mysteriously in Newgate
in September 1798. At 4 o'clock on the morning he was to be
hanged, Tone was found by the 'sentinel who watched in his
room', in his cell, allegedly with a wound to his throat. It
was never established how or by whom the wound was inflicted. He died as a result of the wound on 19 November
1798. He also was thirty-five. Napper Tandy was in France
in 1798 and after an exciting chase around Europe via Ireland, Norway and Ireland again, finally ended up in Bor-
deaux in France in 1801, where he died in 1803. Russell was
held without charge during the rebellion until 1802. He went
to France on his release, whence he returned secretly to help
Robert Emmet in 1803. He was captured in Dublin and
hanged at Downpatrick in November 1803.

Of the remainder, Neilson, McNevin and Thomas Addis
Emmet went to America after release in 1802. Neilson died
of yellow fever the following year. McNevin became pro-
fessor of midwifery and chemistry at the College of Physi-
cians and was appointed resident Physician to the State of
New York. Emmet had a distinguished career at the American Bar, becoming Attorney General to the State of New
York only seven years after arrival. When he died, Governor
Clinton delivered a eulogy over his grave, and a 30-foot-
high marble monument was erected to his memory. Three

more prominent members went to France. Lewins took a university job, and Surgeon Lawless (Lord Edward's friend) rose to be a Major General in the French army. Arthur O'Connor, the last surviving member of the Central Directory, became a naturalised Frenchman, a General-of-Division and a friend of Napoleon. He won a place among the intellectuals, married Eliza, the daughter of the Marquis de Condorcet, sister of Grouchy and intimate of Lafayette. He wrote pamphlets and addresses, edited the *Journal de la Liberté Religieuse*, and lived in a country chateau in the Lorraine, on the pay of a General-of-Division, devoting himself to agriculture and other country pursuits, until his death at an advanced age in 1852.

The United Irishmen failed to win freedom for Ireland by either constitutional agitation or physical force, but they left a legacy of determined resistance to British rule in Ireland which has sustained many a guerrilla fighter from that day to this. Their resistance was smashed by superior military force, and Cornwallis was able to report that 'numberless murders are hourly committed by our people without any process or examination whatever'. Nevertheless, a stand had been made for the first time by inadequately armed country people against the well-armed regular British army, yeomanry and militia, and the mass of the people were encouraged by the spirit of resistance that had been evoked. Time was to show that nothing will ever kill that spirit.

Numberless Murdered

No accurate estimate can be made of the total number of murders committed by the regular troops of the British army and the auxiliary armed forces, yeomanry and militia during the bloody decade of the 1790s but, according to Lecky, Newenham conservatively calculated 'that the direct loss of life during the rebellion alone was about 15,000'. He continues: 'About 1,600 of the King's troops and about 11,000 of the rebels, fell on the field. About 400 loyal persons were massacred or assassinated, and 2,000 rebels were exiled or hanged'. Other estimates were substantially higher.

3

'We are the saints'

The Orange Order

Lamenting in the early eighteenth century on the likelihood
of a union of Catholics and Protestants in the face of action
then under consideration, Primate Boulter wrote the memorable words, 'The worst of this affair is, that it unites Protestants and Papists and if that reconciliation takes place,
farewell to English influence in Ireland'. The illustrious Primate was of course merely restating England's unchanging
Irish policy. 'Should we exert ourselves in reducing this
country to order and civility,' said some of Elizabeth's coun-
sellors, 'it must acquire power, consequence, and riches. The
inhabitants will be thus alienated from England; they will
cast themselves into the arms of some foreign power, or
perhaps erect themselves into an independent and separate
state. Let us rather connive at their disorder; for a weak and
disordered people never can attempt to detach themselves
from the Crown of England'.

England's Irish policy from the beginning was colonial:
acquire the land, confiscate the property of the septs, 'root
out the Irish' from the soil and plant the country systematically with English tenants. 'The idea,' wrote Lecky 'that it
was possible to obtain, at a few hours' or days' journey from
the English coasts, and at little or no cost, great tracts of fertile territory, and to amass in a few years gigantic fortunes,

took hold upon the English mind with a fascination much like that which was exercised by the fables of the exhaustless riches of India in the days of Clive and Hastings'. All were agreed that this policy could be implemented and maintained only by the unswerving backing of the English Government for the colonial garrison, who were put in possession of roughly 80 per cent of the land of Ireland following three successive confiscations and who, with very few exceptions, by the eighteenth century, constituted the Anglican Protestant ascendancy.

Accordingly, all the measures which the garrison introduced during that century to copper-fasten their colonial position and penalise their tenantry – rack-renting, tithes, compulsory labour and the whole unparalleled code of penal oppression, necessarily had to have the full support of the English Government. But they nearly went too far. The severity of their measures provoked anti-landlord associations from tenants of different religious persuasions, such as 'Whiteboys' in the south, 'Oak Boys', and 'Hearts of Steel Boys' in the north. If the owners of property had persisted with their oppression, the result might have been the unification of Catholic and Protestant tenants, with a common anti-landlord bias.

Peep-O-Day Boys and Defenders

Property owners got the message. Reforms were gradually introduced. The worst of the penal laws were allowed to lapse. Catholics, being the principal victims under the code, were, therefore, the principal beneficiaries from its relaxation. Anti-landlord associations accordingly declined for the time being but rival tenant associations soon took their place. Old feuds between poor native tenants and poor planter tenants were revived, particularly in some northern areas. New competition for leases and rents developed. Rivalries between the sects intensified, leading to rows and fights at fairs and wakes, at country sports and in taverns. Fights bred intimidation and more fights. Those in the majority ganged together and began to push out those in the minority. In 1784 an exclusively Protestant association called the Peep-o-Day boys sprang up in Armagh, and appears to have led the way in this campaign. They were subsequently named 'Protestant Boys' and 'Wreckers' and finally 'Orangemen'. The victims of their attacks, mostly Catholics, organised themselves the next year into a group called 'Defenders', purely, as the name implies, as a defensive body.

Battle of the Diamond and the Orange Order

The disturbances between the two bodies rose and fell for a number of years without being the cause of much official concern, but after the foundation of the United Irishmen in 1791, with the declared aim of uniting the different sects and the possibility of a consequent decline in English influence in Ireland should such reconciliation take place, the Government saw the undesirable implications for their own position. They accordingly began to send agents to areas of disturbance to fan the sectarian flames and ensure that the two sides were kept as far apart as possible. A reign of terror is stated to have prevailed in large districts of Ulster. Bodies of several hundred men came into collision on more than one occasion. There were pitched battles in broad daylight. Several lives were lost. The highly agitated feuds came to a head in September 1795 when the two sides met in combat at the Diamond in Armagh and some twenty to thirty Defenders were left dead on the field. The day closed with the founding of the Orange Order.

A report published in the *Edinburgh Review* of January 1836 gives the following account:

> The first Orange lodge was formed on 21 September, 1795, at the house of a man named Sloan, in the obscure village of Loughgall. The immediate cause of those disturbances in the north that gave birth to Orangeism was an attempt to plant colonies of Protestants on the farms or tenements of Catholics who had been forcibly ejected. Numbers of them were seen wandering about the country, hungry, half-naked, and infuriated. Mr Christie, a member of the Society of Friends, who appears to have passed sixty or seventy years on his property

as quietly as a man may in the neighbourhood of such violent neighbours, gives a painful account of the outrages then committed. He says he heard sometimes of twelve or fourteen Catholic houses wrecked in a night and some destroyed: that this 'commenced in the neighbourhood of Churchill, between Portadown and Dungannon, and then it extended over nearly all the northern counties. In the course of time, after the Catholics were many of them driven from the county, and had taken refuge in different parts of Ireland, I understand they went to Connaught. Some years after, when peace and quietness was in a measure restored, some returned again, probably five or six years afterwards. The property which they left was transferred in most instances to Protestants: where they had houses and gardens and small farms of land, it was generally handed over by the landlords to Protestant tenants. That occurred within my knowledge.' He further says: 'It continued for two or three years, but was not quite so bad in 1796 and 1797 as it was earlier. After this wrecking and the Catholics were driven out, what was called 'the Break-of-Day' party merged with Orangeism; they passed from one to the other, and the gentlemen in the county procured what they termed their Orange warrants, to enable them to assemble legally, as they termed it. The name dropped, and Orangeism succeeded to Break-of-Day Men.'

At first the association was entirely confined to the lower orders; but it soon worked its way upwards....

In the words of Lecky, Orangeism was at first, 'simply a form of outrage – the Protestant side of a faction fight which had long been raging in certain counties of the north among the tenants and labourers of the two religions – and the Protestants in Armagh being considerably stronger than the Catholics, Orangeism in that county had assumed the character of a most formidable persecution ... It was a popular and democratic movement, springing up among the lowest classes of Protestants, and essentially lawless'. From being a sort of league of mutual defence among the Protestant lower orders while they were travelling under the names of 'Break of Day Boys', 'Peep-o-Day Boys' or 'Wreckers', it became a secret oath-bound society after adopting the title 'Orange Order' in 1795. It has been generally credited that the oath taken by all the original lodges, continued afterwards to be taken by the lower classes, and was as follows, 'In the awful presence of Almighty God, I, A B, do solemnly swear, that I will, to the utmost of my power, support the King and the present Government; and I do further swear, that I will use my utmost exertions to exterminate all the Catholics of the kingdom of Ireland'.

Initially the upper classes held aloof from the Order and it appears to have been confined almost entirely to Protestant tenants and labourers in Ulster. Shortly, however, the landlords, spotting an advantage to their own ascendancy position, changed their attitudes and placed themselves at the head of the new Order. Under their direction it spread rapidly among the landed gentry, not only in Ulster but throughout the country, and what was at bottom a violently sectarian society thus assumed a veneer of respectability. As subsequent events proved, it gathered into its ranks all the most intolerant and fanatical Protestantism of the country and inherited from its early traditions all the habits of violence and outrage which the new leaders – the landlords – could never wholly repress, even if they wished to do so. At this stage, it was still essentially a small rural organisation: Belfast being but a young commercial centre, with a population of no more than about 20,000.

The English Government also became active in turning the new organisation to its own advantage to counteract the United Irishmen, who were preaching what were to them heretical doctrines: unity among the sects, reform of the ascendancy Parliament, repeal of the remaining penal laws, and giving Catholics the same voting rights as Protestants. Breaches of the law committed by Orangemen were accordingly connived at by the magistrates who were invariably Protestants and mostly Orangemen. No action was taken against members for administering the Orange oath, although United Irishmen were vigorously pursued and punished for administering the United Irish oath. The provisions of the Convention Act and the Insurrection Act were ignored where Orangemen were concerned. Even ordinary criminal offences such as arson, robbery and physical mutilation went unpunished. Under the active encouragement of the Government, the order therefore spread rapidly throughout the country. Members were drawn into the yeomanry and the militia, and existing members of these armed bodies who were in sympathy with the aims of the Orange Society were joining it in increasing numbers. Men who were but up to recently 'Break-of-Day Boys' and 'Wreckers' were now members of the military forces, officered by the ascendancy, and provided with arms which they would shortly use to help the British army destroy the United Irishmen and kill the effort to establish democratic rule in Ireland.

Defenders

On the other hand, the erstwhile opponents of the 'Break-of-Day Boys', the 'Defenders', were being hunted like animals after the so-called battle of the Diamond until the jails were filled with them. About 1,300 were taken from the prisons by Lord Carhampton, without any legal process or form of trial, and sent on board His Majesty's men of war or transport vessels in what was euphemistically described as 'vigour beyond the law', a procedure which enjoyed the protection of an Act of Parliament. From being a simple self-defensive agrarian organisation, the Defenders had now developed into a political body under the influence of United Irishmen teachings, but their objectives do not appear to have been precisely formulated beyond the point of advocating 'that something ought to be done for Ireland'. It is stated that 'they had no persons in their ranks of the upper or even middling class', and that, 'the only man among them above the condition of a labourer was a schoolmaster in Naas of the name of Laurence O'Connor who was executed in 1796'. Napper Tandy was sworn in as a member of the organisation in the same year with a view to bringing it into the United Irishmen, but was apparently informed upon by somebody who was present at the swearing, and had to flee the country. They subsequently merged fully into the United Irishmen and disappeared as a separate organisation.

A few extracts from letters written by British generals serving in Ireland at this time show the new place Orangeism was beginning to take, with the active help of the British Government, a mere year and a half after the founding of the Order. 'I have arranged,' wrote Brigadier-General Knox, 'a plan to scour a district full of unregistered arms ... And this I do, not so much with a hope to succeed to any extent, as to increase the animosity between the Orangemen and the United Irishmen, or liberty men as they call themselves. Upon that animosity depends the safety of the centre counties of the north'. Others urged that the Armagh Orangemen might be organised into a new fencible corps, their loyalty being incontestable. Knox strongly urged the arming of the Orangemen. 'If I am permitted,' he wrote 'as I am inclined, to encourage the Orangemen, I think I shall be able to put down the United Irishmen in Armagh, Monaghan, Cavan, and part of Tyrone'. General Lake begged for permission to seize and burn the *Northern Star*. 'The mischief it does is beyond all imagination ... Belfast ought to be proclaimed and punished most severely, as it is plain every act of sedition originates in this town'. He laments that complete martial law was not proclaimed. 'I cannot help wishing that we had full powers to destroy their houses, or try some of them by our law ... Nothing but terror will keep them in order'.

The success achieved within a couple of years in whipping up sectarianism in the military forces all over the country, as well as in Ulster, is evident from the accounts of the activities of the various regiments of yeomanry and militia in Wexford in 1798, particularly the following account of the North Cork militia by Edward Hay:

> The Orange system made no public appearance in the county of Wexford until the beginning of April, on the arrival of the North Cork militia, commanded by Lord Kingsborough. In this regiment there was a great number of Orangemen, who were zealous in making proselytes and displaying their devices – having medals and Orange ribbons triumphantly pendant from their bosoms. It is believed that previous to this period there were but few actual Orangemen in the county; but soon after, those whose principles inclined that way, finding

themselves supported by the military, joined the association, and publicly avowed themselves by assuming the devices of the fraternity. It is said that the North Cork regiment were also the inventors (but they certainly were the introducers) of pitch–cap torture into the county of Wexford. Any person having his hair cut short (and, therefore, called a croppy, by which appellation the soldiery designated an United Irishman), on being pointed out by some loyal neighbour, was immediately seized and brought into a guardhouse, where caps either of coarse linen or strong brown paper, besmeared inside with pitch, were always kept ready for service. The unfortunate victim had one of these, well heated, compressed on his head, and when judged of a proper degree of coolness, so that it could not be easily pulled off, the sufferer was turned out amidst the horrid acclamations of the merciless torturers; and to the view of vast numbers of people, who generally crowded about the guardhouse door, attracted by the cries of the tormented. Many of those persecuted in this manner experienced additional anguish from the melted pitch trickling into their eyes. This afforded a rare addition of enjoyment to these keen sportsmen, who reiterated their horrid yells of exultation on the repetition of the several accidents to which their game was liable, for, in the confusion and hurry of escaping from the ferocious hands of these more than savage barbarians, the blinded victims frequently fell, or inadvertently dashed their heads against the walls in their way. The pain of disengaging this pitched cap from the head must be next to intolerable. The hair was often torn out by the roots, and not infrequently parts of the skin were so scalded or blistered as to adhere and come off along with it. The terror and dismay that these outrages occasioned are inconceivable.

Tom the Devil

A sergeant of the North Cork, nicknamed Tom the Devil, was most ingenious in devising new methods of torture. Moistened gunpowder was frequently rubbed into the hair which was cut close, and then set on fire. Some, while being shorn for this purpose, had an entire ear and often both ears completely cut off; and many lost part of their noses during the preparation. Yet these atrocities were publicly practised without the least reserve, in open day, and no magistrate or officer ever interfered, but shamefully connived at this extraordinary mode of 'quieting the people'!

No Cursing, Swearing or Intemperance

Although Tom the Devil was most likely an excellent sergeant in the execution of orders given by the magistrates and officers in charge of him, it was unlikely that his brutality and cruelty in terrorising rebels would measure up to the high moral standard laid down in the book of rules and regulations drawn up the very next year by the Reverend S. Cupples, Rector of Lisburn, for circulation among Orangemen. Every Orangeman, it was said, was expected to have a sincere love and veneration for his Maker, and a firm belief in the sole mediatorship of Christ. He must be humane and courteous, and an enemy to all brutality and cruelty; he must abstain from cursing, swearing, and intemperance, and he must carefully observe the Sabbath. The society was exclusively Protestant, and it was based upon the idea of a dominant Protestant nation.

There is no record of what happened to Tom the Devil after Wexford: whether he amended his ways to come up to high Christian standards laid down by the Rev. Cupples or whether, as suspected, he retired to spend many happy years of cursing, swearing and intemperance as an unreformed Orangeman in the North Cork area. His commanding officer, Lord Kingsborough, still under thirty years of age, resigned from the regiment in November 1798 and returned to his stately ancestral castle at Mitchelstown after an undistinguished military career; having lost about one third of his original force of 26 officers, 24 sergeants, 16 drummers, 12 fifers and 446 rank and file in the Wexford fight. Like the Duke of Plaza Toro:

> In enterprise of martial kind,
> When there was any fighting,
> He led his regiment from behind–
> He found it less exciting.

Before the rebellion broke out, the North Cork regiment had assembled at St Stephen's Green to assist the troops in Dublin – the anticipated centre of the rising. As things turned out, the regiment was not required there, because no rising took place in Dublin. Detachments of the unit were, however, engaged elsewhere throughout Leinster during the following weeks, in operations commanded by Captain Swayne, Colonel Foote, Captain Snowe and Lieutenant Bowen – all recognisable ascendancy names in North Cork, and no doubt members of the Orange Order like Kingsborough himself. Meanwhile, the good lord, accompanied by two of his officers, decided to go down from Dublin to Wexford by sea in a hired boat to join his regiment at the rear. When he arrived in Wexford, however, he found the town in the hands of the rebels and himself a prisoner. Were it not for the personal intervention of the rebel commander – Matthew Keogh – it is unlikely that he would ever have got out of Wexford alive, given the brutal record of his largely Orange regiment during the previous two months.

Orangemen Opposed the Union

Although the evangelising of the yeomanry, the militia and the regular forces served England's immediate purpose of promoting antagonism between Catholics and Protestants in order to help destroy the United Irishmen, the Orangemen at the same time were staunch supporters of the exclusively Protestant Parliament in Ireland which Mr Pitt was determined to abolish, regardless of Ireland's wishes. Many of them – including Lord Kingsborough – accordingly voted against the union two years later. They were afraid of losing their ascendancy over Catholics should the latter be granted the same voting rights as themselves in a United Kingdom Parliament, which was being promised in order to secure Catholic support for the proposed union between Ireland and England. After the suppression of the United Irishmen this element saw no reason to put their safe and dominant position at risk. Corps of Yeomen marched, therefore, in processions of protest. Orange lodges passed resolutions in favour of retaining independence. But it was all too late. As far as Mr Pitt was concerned, the union was an imperial necessity, and now that the Orangemen had fulfilled their usefulness in helping him to bring it about, they were expendable.

Subsequent events were to show that the Protestant ascendancy had nothing to fear under the union. In fact it consolidated their entrenched position. Twenty-nine years were to elapse before Catholics could sit in Parliament, and then only at the enormous expense of disfranchising the forty-shilling freeholders. This restricted the right to vote to a mere 14,000 out of a total population of about 7 million. The threat of armed republicanism was removed for many a decade. The Protestants and the Papists were as far apart as any Primate Boulter could desire.

Bribing the Presbyterians

The support given by the republican element among the Presbyterians to the United Irishmen during the previous decade caused such concern that Castlereagh felt compelled to write to his masters in London, 'It is only through a considerable internal fermentation of the body coupled with some change of system that it will put on a different temper and acquire better habits'. Accordingly they set out to bribe the Presbyterian church (as they had already done with the Catholic Church) by substantially increasing the royal bounty called the *Regium Donum* paid to Presbyterian ministers. It was a deliberate move to create division and set one section of the church against another. It had the desired effect. The radical or republican element which supported the United Irishmen lost influence and waned, while the Orange element which supported the Government and the Orange Order prospered.

One of the members from the radical wing, the Rev. Henry Montgomery of Dunmurry, took a liberal stand and in 1813 succeeded in carrying in the Ulster Synod a vote in favour of Catholic Emancipation. In 1829 he spoke from the pulpit in the Catholic church in Donegal in favour of such a measure. His rival from the pro-English wing, Dr Henry

Cooke, threw in his lot with the Tories. He described the liberal traditions of Montgomery and other pre-union reformers as 'leprosy', and declared that those who clung to them 'must have it scourged out or burned out for it will not go out'. In 1829 Montgomery withdrew from the contest to found a separate communion, and left Cooke to frolic away with the Protestant Episcopal church. For all his gesturing, the Presbyterians as a whole seemed to have been shabbily treated by the Tories. No Presbyterian was ever selected for honours. Even wealthy members of the Church were debarred from the magistracy. Presbyterians were still obliged, like Catholics, to pay tithes to the Established Church.

Meanwhile, large numbers of poor Presbyterians as well as poor Protestants of other denominations were being recruited into the Orange Order which was now almost exclusively under landlord and Established church control. Many Presbyterians of the former liberal wing of the Church were coerced into joining under penalty of being branded traitors 'to the cause'. Many others of the disorderly classes, in the tradition of the 'Break-of-Day Boys' and 'Wreckers', joined for the opportunity of exercising power over their Catholic neighbours as their forbears had done for generations. Armed Orange yeomen attended fairs and markets and their presence was usually the cause of conflict. The Arms Acts were not enforced and the Orangemen were given a free hand to create mayhem.

Judge Fletcher once commented about the activities of these Orangemen:

> Murders have been repeatedly perpetrated on such occasions, and though legal prosecutions have ensued, yet such have been the baneful consequences of these factious associations, that, under their influence, petty juries have declined on some occasions to do their duty ... With these Orange associations, I connect all commemorations and processions producing embittering recollections, and inflicting wounds upon the feelings of others; and I do emphatically state it as my settled opinion, that until these associations are effectually put down, and the arms taken from their hands, in vain will the north of Ireland expect tranquillity and peace.

Orange Order Goes 'Fascist'

Within a few decades, Orangeism in England gave rise to a
Parliamentary enquiry and the dissolution of the Order
there. Orange lodges had apparently been established in
most of the British militia and regular units while they were
stationed in Ireland, and HRH the Duke of York, Commander-in-Chief of the army, who is said to have been a
violent Orange partisan, encouraged the process. Even while
still head of the army, he was appointed Orange Grand Master in 1821. He was succeeded in that appointment by his
brother, the Duke of Cumberland – said to have been an
even bigger fanatic. Colonel William Fairman, Grand Secretary and Grand Treasurer of the society in England, was a
close ally of the Duke and concocted a plan to establish him
as Protector should Queen Victoria succeed to the throne
before reaching her maturity. He was relying on the Orange
Society to provide the physical force necessary to break
down any opposition to his scheme. Though Fairman himself was said to have been quite capable of unconstitutional
action, the Orangemen in Britain were not yet considered to
be the full-blooded right-wing authoritarians needed for
such an audacious operation.

The Poor and Ignorant Orangemen

The Government became alarmed and a Parliamentary Select Committee was set up in 1835 to enquire into the whole
affair. In their report the Committee declared *inter alia*:

> It is notorious that the Orange Lodges exist under the pat-
> ronage of men high in rank in England, Ireland and Scotland,
> and the countenance given, in consequence of all the orders of
> the Orange institution being issued by and under the authority
> of such men as His Royal Highness the Duke of Cumberland,
> as Imperial Grand Master, and of His Grace the Duke of Gor-
> don, Deputy Grand Master for Scotland, will be found to have
> a greater effect on the poor and ignorant – of which the
> Orangemen chiefly consist – than might be expected.

Following the issue of the report, the society was dissolved in England at the request of King William IV and was not re-constituted until 1845. It still continued in Ireland. Its membership at the time of dissolution was estimated at 200,000.

In the middle of the century, England again made good use of the Orange card to scotch a budding unity between Catholic and Protestant tenants. The Marquess of London-derry complained, 'Orangemen and Catholics have united together to obtain a reduction of rents, tenant right, and fixity of tenure, and not only to do that, but to force their landlords by intimidation to accede to those objects'. Northern tenants established a Tenants' Association in 1848, and linked up with the Southern Societies in 1850 in a new all-Ireland organisation known as the League of North and South. It was a hopeful movement. One of the liberal Presbyterian ministers declared, 'All the old animosities were forgotten, buried in oblivion, and whoever attempted to disinter them ought to be considered as the most infamous of "resurrectionists"'. But England's rulers, never slow to see the danger to their influence in Ireland in a unity between Protestants and Catholics, quickly produced the wedge to drive them apart again. Lord John Russell introduced the Ecclesiastical Titles Bill and raised the cry of 'No Popery'. It was enough to rouse 'all the old animosities' again, and the issue of fair rents and tenant rights for the unfortunate tenants of Ireland now became of mere secondary importance. Dr Wiseman had recently been made Catholic Archbishop of Westminster and the dilemma of whether that title should be tolerated in Protestant England seemed far more relevant to many churchmen.

Religion as an Economic Weapon

The suggestion often made that the Orange Order was founded to keep alive the principles of the Whig revolution of 1688, or to commemorate King William of pious and immortal memory, is entirely inaccurate. The truth is, of course, that the Order was founded by poor Protestant tenants in Sloan's house near Loughall in 1795 to protect and expand their material interests against even poorer Catholic tenants. It had nothing whatever to do with the Whig revolution or King William. Just as the penal code had to be wrapped up in religious garb to conceal the fact that it was framed to protect the ascendancy in their ill-gotten confiscated properties, religious motive had also to be found now to conceal the fact that the primary aim of the Orange Order was economic. The argument that Papists were believers in false and evil doctrines was used to provide the necessary religious camouflage.

It was specious argument of this sort, widely disseminated by mob agitators – Henry Cooke, Thomas Drew, Hugh Hanna and a host of others – that greatly exacerbated the antagonism between Protestants and Catholics. Those who like to present the Order as a respectable, well-intentioned body, have written that in the early nineteenth century few men of education or standing belonged to it, and complained that lodge meetings and anniversary celebrations were simply occasions for excessive drinking and disseminating anti-papist propaganda. Nevertheless, during that period, a widespread organisation was built up with local lodges affiliated to County Lodges and a Grand Central Lodge all under the control of a 'Grand Black Chapter', an 'Imperial Grand Master' and a 'Grand Council'.

Street Politics

The first important occasion since the union in which the economic objective was called into play, and the Orange Order was manipulated by British politicians for their own ends, was in 1886 when Gladstone made his first move to grant a relatively minor measure of Home Rule to Ireland. No sooner had Gladstone introduced his Bill, than Lord Randolph Churchill, who had been a member of the recently defeated Tory Government, crossed over to Ireland and urged the Orangemen in the Ulster Hall in Belfast to use force if necessary to defeat the lawfully elected Government – allegedly to protect their own interests. 'Now may be the time,' he told them, 'to show whether all these ceremonies and forms which are practised in your Orange lodges are really living symbols or idle and meaningless shibboleths'. He was determined to use whatever tactics were necessary to get Gladstone out of power and the Tories back into office. That it was no hasty step, but rather a carefully thought out move, is clear from a passage in his letter to a friend:

> I decided some time ago that if Gladstone went for Home Rule the Orange Card was the one to play. Please God it may turn out to be the ace of trumps and not the two....

Every word Churchill uttered was seditious but he was neither censured by the House of Commons nor expelled from the Privy Council as threatened. The agitation generated by him led to street riots and mob violence in Belfast. Many were killed and hundreds were wounded. His allies, such as roaring Hanna, called forth deep fears of Catholic domination and warned that Home Rule meant Rome Rule. Nobody explained to the Orange mob that the Pope was 100 per cent unionist and pro-British; that the Church had given King Henry II and all his successors in title the whole island of Ireland in the famous Bull *Laudabiliter* seven hundred years before; that a pope had sided with the Orange King Billy of pious and immortal memory at the Battle of the Boyne and had sung *Te Deums* in Rome after King Billy's victory; that all the Catholic Bishops supported the Act of Union when Orange lodges were passing resolutions in favour of retaining an Irish Parliament in Dublin; and that republicanism had its origin in the liberal wing of the Presbyterian Church. In Churchill's scheme of things, all of that counted for nothing. He had roused the mobs in Belfast. A number of Gladstone's own party deserted him. The Home Rule Bill was defeated. Gladstone was out. The Tories were back in power with Churchill as Chancellor of the Exchequer.

We are the Saints

Following Churchill's exploitation of the Orange Card, the

Orange Order prospered immensely. Large numbers of wealthy business and professional people, clergymen of all Protestant denominations, and middle classes as well as landlords, joined up and came into positions of control. Descendants of the Peep-o-Day Boys, artisans and ordinary workers, who constituted the Order at its foundation in 1795, also joined. However, whereas their forefathers had actively fought their Protestant masters for better conditions and had won rights known as 'the Ulster custom', well ahead of the Land League's winning of similar rights for tenants in other parts of Ireland, the new members of the Order were much more quiescent under equally bad conditions.

From pulpit and platform, Protestants were warned about the threat to their own positions should any concessions be made to Catholics. It was pointed out that their best protection lay in membership of the Orange Order which existed to safeguard their interests against Catholics. All the loyal Orangeman needed, they were assured, was:

> The crown of the causeway in road and in street,
> And the Papishes under my feet.

Given the ease with which fanaticism of this sort could be whipped up by Orange propagandists, Ulster employers soon learned how to divide their workforce through a systematic policy of discrimination against Catholics, especially in the better areas of employment – shipbuilding, engineering and manufacturing. Under such conditions, no effective trade union movement which would bring about a fair system of recruitment and promotion could be developed.

The chief beneficiaries under this system were, of course, the Orange employers themselves. They could, as a result of their carefully worked out discriminatory procedures, keep wages low and profits high. Like the grim-faced, black-hatted Puritan colonists in America when they first laid covetous eyes on the fertile lands of Massachusetts (then occupied by a few defenceless Indians), it is most probable that the pious Orange capitalists of the nineteenth and twentieth centuries, 'In bowler hats and Sunday suits, Orange sashes, polished boots', called a meeting, and after opening with suitable religious solemnity, in order to give the sanctimonious air of religion to their proceedings, resolved:

> That the Earth is the Lord's, and the fullness thereof.
>> That the Lord hath given the Earth as an inheritance unto his saints....

and then, no doubt, behind closed doors, resolved *that we are the saints.*

What a Fool I was

Speaking in the House of Lords on 14 December 1921 – eight days after the signing of the Anglo-Irish Treaty – Edward Carson, the father of Orange subversion in this century, expressed his bitter disillusionment at the way he had been duped and manipulated by British politicians:

> I was in earnest. I was not playing politics. I believed all this. What a fool I was. I was only a puppet and so was Ulster, and so was Ireland in the political game that was to get the Conservative Party into power.

What he was saying was true of course, but it was too late for regrets. He had become part of a massive conspiracy by the Tories to get the Liberals out of office in England and to get themselves back into power.

No sooner had the Liberal Government introduced its third Home Rule Bill in 1912 than the Tories decided to play the Orange card once again for all it was worth. A campaign of intimidation and subversion began at once. Bonar Law – the leader of the party, F.E. Smith – later Lord Birkenhead, Walter Long, Austen Chamberlain and a whole army of senior Tory politicians, former ministers of state, field marshals, generals, admirals, past and prospective office holders of whom few had anything to do with or any knowledge of Irish affairs, descended on Ulster. At one stage there were no less than seventy senior Tories campaigning in Belfast and its environs. They openly incited armed rebellion. They urged the Orangemen to sign the Covenant and to join the private army which was being organised and armed in Ulster and in England under the command of an English general. They preached subversion in the Commons and in the constituencies. 'If Ulster does resist by force,' said Bonar Law in the Commons on 18 June 1912, 'there are stronger influences than Parliamentary majorities'. 'There is no length to which Ulster would not be entitled to go, however desperate and unconstitutional,' said Birkenhead at Liverpool. And at Nottingham he pronounced, 'They [the Orangemen] will have the full support, not only of the unionists of Ireland but of the whole of the unionist members of the House of Commons in all risks, in all hazards, and in every extremity'.

Winston Churchill (son of Lord Randolph Churchill), then First Lord of the Admiralty in the Liberal Government, poured scorn on the hypocrisy of the Tories in their 'concern' for minority rights in Ireland: 'They have always been straining for some short cut to office and they now seek to utilise the fanaticism of the Orangemen ... Behind every sentence of Bonar Law's speeches on the Ulster question, there was the whispering of the party [Tory] manager, "We must have an election. Ulster is our best card. It is our only card. This is our one chance"'. Churchill had every reason to know all about Tory chicanery in relation to the Orangemen. He was a member of the Liberal team who had been negotiating with them with a view to forming a coalition Government after the indecisive general election of 1911. On that occasion, that most rabid Tory anti-Home Ruler – Birkenhead – was prepared to abandon his opposition to Home Rule and ditch the Orangemen, in order to get into power. 'What a world we live in,' commented his Tory colleague, Austen Chamberlain, 'and how the public would stare if they could look into our minds and letter bags'.

J.B. Armour, the Presbyterian minister from Ballymoney castigated those who had been stirring up religious hatred.

'Some of those who are exploiting the persecuting bogey for political ends,' he said 'have not much religion to persecute. To their credit, Irish Catholics have never been known to persecute for religious beliefs ... I have no fear for true Protestantism in the future, either in Ireland or elsewhere, though political Protestantism has had its day'. 'The bureaucracy which is ruling Ireland,' he added, 'is largely Protestant. The fear that the management of the state machinery will not remain in the hands of the descendants of the ascendancy party is perhaps the strongest factor in opposition to Home Rule'.

However, the subversion of the Tories for their own political ends continued apace. They conspired with senior army officers to paralyse from within the disciplined action of the army; they plotted with General Sir Henry Wilson, Director of Military Operations at the War Office (and later Chief of the Imperial General Staff) to ensure that the projected illegal importation of arms into Ulster, financed in part by Tory funds, would not be interfered with by the authorities; they engineered the plan that British army officers stationed at the Curragh would refuse to move if ordered north; they planned to get the House of Lords to refuse to pass the Annual Army Bill which would mean that there would be no army at all in existence after 30 April 1914; they suborned the press; and finally, they secretly collaborated in the successful landing of 35,000 rifles and 2,500,000 rounds of ammunition at Larne on 24 April 1914.

The whole conspiracy had been designed to force the Liberals out of office as in 1886. But the Government did not resign. In the face of the challenge engineered in Ulster and the politically organised disaffection in the army, they simply abandoned their Home Rule Bill which had now gone through nearly all stages up to getting the Royal Assent. A mere eighteen days after the landing of arms in Larne, Lloyd George, Chancellor of the Exchequer, announced to the Commons that before the Home Rule Bill came into operation an amending Bill excluding part of Ulster would be introduced. Subversion had won the day. Partition was born.

This, however, was not the end for which the Tories had worked. By their effective playing of the Orange card, they had hoped to be able to drive the Liberals from office, and had there been an early general election they would most likely have succeeded as in 1886. The Great War intervened, however, and the Tories were forced to share power with the Liberals and Labour for another six years. It was not until 1922 that the Tory party was able to form a Government on its own under Bonar Law. Neither was partition the end sought by Carson. That was why he felt cheated. He merely wanted to kill Home Rule and keep all Ireland in the union. Instead, under the Government of Ireland Act 1920, he was given Home Rule for a mutilated country. Neither he nor any other Irish representative voted for the Act when it was going through the Commons on 11 November 1920.

The unwanted outcome to the whole conspiracy was the elevation of the provincial Orange Order, founded by the 'Peep-o-Day Boys' and 'Wreckers', to the status of an Orange state which placed all power in the hands of one sector of the community, and which opened a new chapter in police state methods, gerrymandering, economic apartheid, and bloody repression by police and regular troops of the British army.

4

'Hell is not hot enough'

The Fenians

Unlike the United States of America, held to have been 'conceived in liberty and dedicated to the proposition that all men are created equal', the union between Great Britain and Ireland in 1800 was conceived in force and dedicated to the proposition that Ireland is and always must remain subject to Great Britain. Britain perceived it to be a strategic need to safeguard her western flank. It was not, therefore, a union at all, but simply the forceful annexation by a big power of a small neighbouring country, like the annexation in 1990 of Kuwait by Iraq.

Acquisition of Ireland by force involved as a corollary the continued use of force to maintain it in subjection. England, therefore, set out from the start of the union to reduce Ireland to her own image and likeness – the weaker sister of a pair of isles, to be known henceforth as the 'British Isles'.

Social policy was directed towards the suppression of every manifestation of Ireland's separate national identity. The teaching of Irish history and of the Irish language was banned in the state schools although Irish was the only language many of the pupils could understand. A sustained effort was made to instil into Irish children the belief that they should be thankful that God had smiled on their birth and caused them to be born as 'happy English children'.

Economic policy was framed to ensure that all requirements of manufactured goods would be supplied by British manufacturers rather than by native industry, and that Irish agricultural workers would be forced, because of the absence of an alternative market, to supply Britain's industrial population with food, at the lowest possible world prices. The end result was unrelieved misery for Ireland.

The policies adopted caused over-taxation, poverty for agricultural producers and dwellers in towns and villages dependent on agriculture, lack of industrial opportunity for residents in the bigger urban centres, famine and ongoing emigration. As Sir Anthony McDonnell, one time Under-Secretary for Ireland said in his evidence before the Primrose Committee, 'The over-weight in taxation had gone on from the date of the union, while the people were becoming gradually enfeebled and their taxable capacity growing less and less ... A number equal to the whole population of the country has been cleared out, and that, I submit, is a result which is a scandal to British administration. They would not have gone if they could have lived in their own country'. England could thus look forward to that happy day when, in the words of *The Times*, 'A Catholic Celt will be as rare on the banks of the Shannon as a Red Indian on the shores of Manhattan', when the majority of the native population would be cowed into subjection and the remainder would be corrupted into West British collaborators.

America, Canada, Australia and Britain itself were to become the new homelands for the floods of Irish emigrants both before and after the Great Famine. Those who remained were forced to accept whatever opportunities were available – jobs in teaching, in the RIC, in the British legal system, in the service of landlords and other members of the Establishment or as tenants at will and labourers on the land, under appalling conditions.

There was near general agreement that the union was a disaster, but there was no agreement as to how it could be undone. For many years, Daniel O'Connell, the leading Irish politician in the first half of the nineteenth century, maintained that Britain could be persuaded by force of argument to repeal the union. He argued that if Catholic Emancipation could be extorted by peaceful agitation, the same weapon could be used successfully to force Britain to repeal the Union. However, there was a fundamental difference between the two questions as far as Britain was concerned. Catholic Emancipation represented no loss whatever to Britain. It was in fact a positive gain. It actually consolidated the 'British Empire'. By giving the mass of Catholics the illusion of freedom it brought the Catholic Church and millions of ordinary members more completely within her power, while at the same time it opened up high official positions to the wealthier and educated Catholics. Repeal of the union, however, would represent a definite loss for Britain, in strategic and financial terms.

While Britain believed that her strategic interests required that Ireland should be kept under her control, no amount of peaceful agitation was going to induce her to repeal the union. On the contrary, all the resources of the Empire would be used to preserve it, even if that meant that Ireland should be 'drowned in blood'. Englishmen of all sorts, of all parties and of all creeds regarded repeal as a mortal stab at the heart of the Empire and were fully resolved to resist it at all costs.

For years, the English press mocked all constitutional agitation for repeal and the matter was never mentioned in Parliament save with a jeer. 'Whatever might be the inconvenience or disadvantage,' wrote *The Times*, 'or even unwholesome restraint upon Ireland – although the union secures the reverse of these – but even were it gall to Ireland, England must guard her own life's blood, and sternly tell the disaffected Irish: "you shall have me for a sister or a subjugatrix; this is my ultimatum".' *The Morning Chronicle* wrote 'True, it was coarsely and badly done, but stand it must. A Cromwell's violence, with Machiavelli's perfidy, may have been at work; but the treaty after all is more than parchment'.

O'Connell's effort to secure repeal by peaceful agitation

reached its climax in 1843. His final monster repeal meeting was fixed for Sunday, 8 October, on the shore by Clontarf. The Government proclaimed it on Saturday afternoon after tens of thousands who were due to gather there from all parts of the country had actually left home and were well on the road. Rather than risk the casualties that would ensue from an Amritsar-type confrontation with the British military, O'Connell called off the meeting at the last moment and had the crowds turned back. It marked the end of his effort to secure repeal by peaceful means. A new generation of men – the Young Irelanders – preaching that the union could only be undone by physical force, had sprung up. The more militant among them maintained that the proclamation banning the Clontarf meeting should have been ignored and that even if the troops fired on the unarmed multitudes that day, the deaths of five or six thousand might have ended the union and saved Ireland from the hundreds of thousands of deaths shortly afterwards in the Great Famine and its sequel.

It was Britain's handling of the Famine and its consequences, however, that ultimately decided for many, who were not overawed by the overwhelming odds against them, that Britain's grip on Ireland would have to be broken, and that there was no way this could be done save by equally determined physical opposition.

Eight million Irish people were now deemed to be subjects of the United Kingdom. Britain claimed full *de facto* and *de jure* control over them. She maintained 140,000 armed troops and 12,000 to 14,000 armed police in the country to back up her claim. She legislated for them, taxed them and punished them under a series of unprecedented coercive measures. Speaking in the House of Lords on 23 March 1846, Earl Grey repeated the list of coercive measures passed since 1800: 'how, in 1800, the Habeas Corpus Act was suspended, the Act for the Suppression of the Rebellion being still in force; how coercion was renewed in 1801; continued again in 1804; how the Insurrection Act was passed in 1807, which gave the Lord-Lieutenant full power to place any district under martial law, to suspend trial by jury and make it a transportable offence to be out of doors from sunset to sunrise; how this Act remained in force till 1810; how it was renewed in 1814 – continued in 1815, 1816, 1817 – revived in 1822, and continued through 1823, 1824, and 1825; how another Insurrection Act was needed in 1833, was renewed in 1834, and expired but five years ago. And again in 1846, we are called on to renew it'.

Yet, Britain allowed two million of her subjects, or roughly 25 per cent of the total Irish population for which she claimed responsibility, to die of hunger and disease on her own doorstep while there were enough grain and animal products available in the country to feed the entire population twice over.

It was accepted that Britain was not responsible for the failure of the potato crop, but she was entirely responsible for the deaths from the consequences of that failure in a part of her kingdom no further away from the seat of power than Yorkshire – and closer than Scotland. Had the blight and famine occurred in the South of France, the whole revenue of that country would have been employed in organising public works, purchasing and distributing corn and other food supplies until the distress was over. Had Yorkshire or Lancashire or any part of England suffered a like calamity, the Government would, without doubt, have promptly taken such measures as were necessary to deal with it. In fact, potatoes failed all over Europe during the 1840s, but there was no famine anywhere except in Ireland.

For a long time of course, Britain had been concerned with the problem of ridding Ireland of its surplus population. She set up a commission of landlords in 1843 under Lord Devon to make recommendations. 'You might as well', remarked O'Connell, 'consult butchers about keeping Lent, as consult these men about the rights of farmers'. In 1845, just before the first great failure of the potato, they made their report. They recommended that small farms should be consolidated and that a proportion of the surplus population of about one million people should be removed – that is,

swept out on the highways, where their choice would be
America, the poor house, or the grave. They also proposed
state-aided emigration to the colonies and a scheme to resettle people on mountains, bogs and wastelands. 'Remove
Irishmen,' wrote *The Times*, 'to the Ganges or the Indus – to
Delhi, Benares or Trincomalee – and they would be far more
in their element than in a country to which an inexorable
fate has confined them'. The landlords would have nothing
to do, however, with the proposal to resettle people on the
four million acres of available wastelands. These were badly
wanted for snipe shooting. Accordingly, they resisted the
bill to give effect to the commissioners' proposal; and English landlords on principle, supported them in their resistance. To such people the Famine was God's answer to their
prayers. They would never again have to worry about Ireland's surplus population.

While those in the western part of the new United Kingdom, namely the Irish, were thus dying like flies during the
years of the Great Hunger, those in the eastern part of the
kingdom, namely 'the English people and working classes'
were, according to the financial statement issued in February
1847 by Sir Charles Wood, Chancellor of the Exchequer,
'steadily growing more comfortable, nay more luxurious in
their style of living'. Increased consumption could not, he
added, 'be accounted for by attributing it to the higher and
wealthier classes, but must have arisen from the consumption of the large body of the people and the working classes.'
'In the matter of coffee,' he went on, 'they had used nearly
seven million pounds of it more than they did in 1843. Of
butter and cheese they devoured double as much within the
year as they had done three years before within the same
period. Of currants ... the quantity used by the "body of the
people and working classes" had increased in three years,
from 254,000 hundred-weight to 359,000 hundred-weight by
the year. Of tea, consumption had increased by £5,400,000
since 1843 ... They had as much beef and bacon as they
could eat, and bread a discretion, and beer!' Clearly, it was
the land of Ireland, not its people, that Britain wanted.

The specific relief measures introduced at the time are worth mentioning. A paltry sum of around £10 million was lent by the Government to the Public Works and Public Commissariat Departments on the security of the rates. However, the schemes this sum was meant to cover were so incompetently and corruptly administered by the 10,000 officials employed to organise the work, that the greater part of the intended benefit never reached the hungry at all. In addition, as if pouring salt on the wounds of the starving, Prime Minister Peel repealed the corn laws in 1846 and proposed the abolition of duty on foreign beef, mutton and bacon, thereby making food for the English consumer cheaper, while impoverishing the Irish producer still further.

Early in 1847, Her Majesty Queen Victoria subscribed £2,000 to an Association set up in England (The British Association) for the relief of distress in Ireland. It represented one-tenth of a penny per person or £1 per thousand of those who died of hunger during the Famine. Parnell made reference to her contribution in the course of a speech made by him during his tour of America in 1880 – thirty-three years later. He was attacked in the press in England, and in certain Irish journals. Lord Randolph Churchill attempted to contradict his statement to which Parnell replied as follows in the *New York Herald*:

In reference to Lord Randolph Churchill's contradiction of my statements, that the Queen gave nothing to relieve the Famine in 1847, I find I might have gone still further and have said with perfect accuracy, that not only did she give nothing, but that she actually intercepted £6,000 of the donation which the Sultan of Turkey desired to contribute to the Famine fund. In 1847 the Sultan had offered a donation of £10,000, but the English Ambassador at Constantinople was directed by the Queen to inform him that her contribution was to be limited to £2,000, and that the Sultan should not, in good taste, give any more than her Majesty; hence the net result to the Famine fund by the Queen's action was a loss of £6,000. All this is perfectly understood by students of Irish history, and would have been known to Lord R. Churchill were our history not proscribed in English schools. The following passage in D'Arcy Magee's history of the Irish settlers in North America throws additional light upon the subject:

> The Czar, the Sultan, and the Pope sent their rubies and their pearls. The Pasha of Egypt, the Shah of Persia, the Emperor of China, the Rajahs of India, combined to do for Ireland what her so-styled rulers refused to do – to keep her young and old people living in the land. America did more than all the rest of the world.
>
> Charles S Parnell.
> 1 February, 1880

The turning point arrived when in the last year of the Famine, hundreds of thousands were perishing in the midst of plenty and it became clear that it was British policy to let the Famine run its course and let it do what Britain's own ad hoc scorched earth policies had so often unsuccessfully attempted in the past. Many people could now see that, in order to protect herself, Ireland had no option but to secure the repeal of the union and set up her own Government. Britain had made it clear, however, that she would never allow that to happen even if it meant drowning Ireland in blood. The only alternative, therefore, for those who were not prepared to submit to that fate, was revolt.

The first of such revolts was the token insurrection by the Young Irelanders under the leadership of William Smith O'Brien at Ballingarry, Co. Tipperary on 5 August 1848. Militarily, a hopelessly unorganised attempt without specific objectives, it could not be called an insurrection at all. But it was led by men of integrity and represented the thin edge of the physical force wedge which widened into the much bigger effort by the Fenians ten years later and the still greater and more effective effort fifty years later again – in 1916–21. In reply to the Young Irelanders, Sir Robert Peel decided that what Ireland needed was not freedom at all, but a new coercion bill which would make her national aspirations not only a crime, but an ignominious crime, on a footing with arson, forgery and waylaying with intent to murder. His bill was duly passed into 'law' and thereafter anybody advocating repeal of the union was to be treated as a 'felon'.

Despite the failure of the 1848 revolt, the tradition of physical resistance to British rule put down vigorous roots for the self-evident reason expressed by Lord Chesterfield a century earlier, that man has a natural right to liberty and good usage and that, when he is 'oppressed and provoked to a certain degree', he 'will and ought to rebel'. It is the same as the Jefferson dictum in the American Declaration of Independence that 'when a long train of abuses and usurpations, pursuing invariably the same object, evinces a design to reduce them (the people) under absolute despotism, it is their right, it is their duty, to throw off such government, and to provide new guards for their future security'.

Conditions were undoubtedly bad in Ireland during the eighteenth century, but nothing could match, much less surpass the universal ill-usage, abuse and oppression of the Irish people in the mid-nineteenth century, when James Stephens, John O'Mahony and other survivors from the 1848 revolt set up the Fenian organisation. Some 2 million people or roughly 25 per cent of the total population had been wiped out over a few years, and tens of thousands were fleeing the country as fast as they could find transport. The answer of the Government to their problems was not food but more military, more police and more coercion.

Her Majesty declared that atrocious crimes were being committed in Ireland by starving people who had the temerity to take even elementary steps to feed their dependents. There was a spirit of insubordination and organised resistance to 'legal rights' abroad, she said, and stern measures were required to protect human lives, that is the lives of landlords, bailiffs and other oppressors, not the lives of the hungry. So, under new coercion laws, disturbed districts were to be proclaimed and once proclaimed everybody in that district had to be within doors (whether he had a house or not) from dusk until dawn. Anybody found not at home was to be arrested and transported. All the arms in a proclaimed district were to be handed in, and if arms were found in any man's premises and he could not prove that they were put there without his knowledge, he was liable to arrest, imprisonment or transportation. The Lord Lieutenant could quarter on the district as many police, inspectors, detectives and sub-inspectors as he might think fit, charge all the expense upon the tenantry, not the landlords, and get the constabulary to collect the additional rates at the point of the bayonet.

'I conceive,' said William Smith O'Brien in the Commons when this latest piece of coercion was being imposed on a grossly abused people, 'that it is the peculiar duty of the Irish people to obtain the possession of arms at a time when you tell them you are prepared to crush their expression of opinion, not by argument, but by brute force'. Coming from one who was himself a member of the landed class and a moderate man this was enough to make other landlords, mortgagees and insurance officers tremble for their gains. When Her Majesty had nothing better to offer the hungry but more jails, more handcuffs and more transportation, it became increasingly clear to all those who desired freedom from British rule that they had no alternative but to fight for it.

The reluctant acceptance by many people of the alternative of force, after the long period of unfulfilled hope generated by O'Connell's spell-binding but ultimately inadequate oratory, and the disillusionment following the recent betrayal by the two members of the constitutional Independent Irish Party – Sadlier and Keogh – account in part at least, for the relatively rapid spread of the Irish Republican Brotherhood (IRB), otherwise known as the Fenians.

The Fenians had no other objective but the undoing of the union by physical force and the establishment of an Irish Republic. The secret oath of their organisation ran: 'I, A B, in the presence of Almighty God, do solemnly swear allegiance to the Irish Republic now virtually established; and that I will do my very utmost, at every risk, while life lasts, to defend its independence and integrity; and finally, that I will yield implicit obedience in all things, not contrary to the law of God, to the commands of my superior officers. So help me God. Amen.'

They were, in effect, a secret guerilla army organised in circles on a pattern familiar on the continent, where Stephens and O'Mahony had got the idea. Each circle theoretically consisted of 820 men made up in multiples of nine and commanded by a Centre. Under each Centre were nine Bs or captains, and under each B were nine Cs or sergeants, each of whom commanded nine men or Ds. In practice, this neat mathematical arrangement was rarely achieved and the strength of different Circles often varied widely. The general aim that members should only know the men in their own section was also attainable only to a limited extent.

Unlike the Whiteboys and other agrarian guerilla organisations which grew out of conflict between tenant farmers, cottiers and the landlords, and whose aims were essentially economic, the objective of the Fenian movement was almost entirely political and it drew its support mainly (but with a certain amount of overlapping between urban and rural areas) from among working men – small farmers and labourers, clerks, shop assistants, mechanics, craftsmen and artisans. The broader objective of the movement and the additional population sectors from which support was drawn, were other factors accounting for the rapid spread of the organisation over the next few years, both at home and among the Irish abroad. Practically every town and village in Ireland had a Fenian branch and Irish emigrants in America and Britain were also recruited in substantial numbers. It has been estimated that there were some 80,000 enrolled in Ireland alone by 1864/1865 and many more thousands in Britain and America. Along with John Boyle O'Reilly and Patrick 'Pagan' O'Leary, John Devoy is said to have enrolled some 15,000 Irish soldiers serving in the British army.

In terms of numbers this was a substantial force, but it was largely unarmed and without military training. The general idea was that arms and training personnel would come from America when the time for action arrived. This, however, was only partly fulfilled. At the conclusion of the American civil war in 1865 considerable numbers of officers trained in the war arrived to take on the training of the

Fenians at home, but owing to conflict in the organisation in America the promised arms did not arrive. The result was fatal to Fenian plans. The Rising planned for 1865 had to be postponed. When it did eventually occur on the night of 4-5 March 1867, after a number of intervening postponements, the Government, through its extensive network of spies, was well aware of the whole conspiracy, and most of the Fenian leaders were already behind prison bars. The limited outbreaks which did take place occurred mainly in Dublin and Cork and at a number of small centres elsewhere in Leinster and Munster. Connaught and Ulster were not affected. Police barracks were attacked at Tallaght and Kilmallock but the attackers were miserably armed and had no success.

Like the Insurrection of 1848, the revolt was little more than a gesture and was over almost before it got started. Total casualties on both sides were estimated at about twelve. Later in the year (September) three members of the organisation – Allen, Larkin and O'Brien – were hanged at Manchester for their part in an attack on a prison van conveying Colonel Thomas Kelly, head of the IRB, which resulted in the accidental shooting of one of the police guards, Sergeant Brett. An explosion in December, of a barrel of gunpowder outside the wall of Clerkenwell prison, in an attempt to rescue two Fenian prisoners detained therein, marked the end of the physical force effort for that year.

The failure of the risings of 1848 and 1867 led many to feel that, given the odds, physical force could hardly be any more successful than peaceful agitation in forcing Britain to relinquish its grip on Ireland. There was criticism from many quarters particularly from those who regarded the union as a good thing in itself and had no wish to see it undone one way or another. The Catholic Church was particularly scathing. Most of the Fenians were Catholics and all the censure and spiritual deprivation which the Church could conjure up was heaped on their heads – denunciation from the altar, refusal of the sacraments, threat of eternal damnation and even excommunication. In the course of a notorious sermon from the altar of Killarney Cathedral on 9

March 1867 – only days after the failed rising in Kerry where one policeman was killed – His Lordship the Most Reverend Dr Moriarty, Bishop of Kerry, declared that the Fenians 'had resisted the ordinance of God and by so doing, they purchased for themselves damnation'. In his condemnation of what he called the heads of the conspiracy he exclaimed :

> O God's heaviest curse, His withering, blasting, blighting curse is on them ... When we look down into the fathomless depth of this infamy, of the heads of the Fenian conspiracy, we must acknowledge that eternity is not long enough, nor hell hot enough, to punish such miscreants.

His Eminence Cardinal Cullen had made clear his attitude towards physical force as far back as 1861 when he refused to allow the remains of the veteran Young Irelander, Terence Bellew McManus, into the Pro-Cathedral or any church in his diocese for a funeral service. The body had been brought home from California and on being refused admission to any church building was removed to the Mechanics' Institute from which the burial service was then conducted. Sixteen years later the remains of the old Fenian, John O'Mahony, were brought back from New York and the procedure was repeated. Again, the body would not be allowed into any church building in the diocese of Dublin, and the funeral service took place from the Mechanics' Institute. Writing in connection with the McManus funeral on 10 November 1861, the Cardinal (then Archbishop of Dublin) stated:

> Some lunatic decided to bring the remains home to arouse a revolutionary spirit and a committee of Protestants, Catholics and the people of no religion were formed ... There was a large funeral, mostly artisans and mechanics; the Catholics of standing abstained.

The decisions and remarks of the cardinal confirm not alone his attitude towards physical force but more particularly the class division in the Catholic Church in Ireland at that time. 'Artisans and mechanics' were a different class of Catholics from 'Catholics of standing'. The Fenian organisation consisted of course mainly of 'artisans and mechanics' and other members of the working classes – labourers, shop assistants, small farmers – all employed in poorly-paid occupations. 'Catholics of standing', who would have nothing to do with the Fenians, were drawn from the well-to-do middle classes – professional and business people and better-off farmers. Commenting on the attitude of the better-off classes towards the Fenian effort, one who had close family connections with some of the surviving members of the organisation wrote:

> It is a difficult matter for a rich man to appreciate the courage and selflessness of a seemingly ineffectual effort by poor men, and so the Fenians were misunderstood by the well-intentioned but thoughtless, and despised in the homes of those whose only criterion of effort is success, whose only standard of success is material advancement.

The same writer remembers the Fenians he knew as a child as 'strangely humble, strangely quiet, strangely reticent'. One or two were British soldiers who had been in the Crimean war and he was puzzled about reconciling membership of the organisation with taking the queen's shilling until he heard of John Devoy and 'Pagan' O'Leary. He recalled, 'Most of them had lived as boys through the grim Famine years. Mitchel was one of their heroes ... Meagher, too, they admired ... but Captain Mackey was the man they most loved ... conditions being as they were in the Ireland of their boyhood, most must have known poverty and privation'. In the light of their betrayal by 'the unspeakable Sadlier ... and the renegade John Keogh', and by the cynical attitude of politicians who 'thanked God they had a country to sell', he could understand why the old Fenians he knew 'were disillusioned, bewildered, hopeless; depressed because of failure, subdued because they had had their fill of victimisation, reticent because of training and distrustful of politics because of their experience'.

The attitude of the Catholic Church towards the Fenians was understandable because it was largely dictated by its own political outlook for over a century. Being aware of the treatment meted out to the Church in France at the time of the French Revolution, the Irish Church was somewhat frightened of the first Republican organisation – The United Irishmen – which sprang up shortly afterwards and appeared to be steeped in the French principles of *Liberté*, *Égalité* and *Fraternité*. There was, however, no comparison between the entrenched position of the continental Church and the much weaker Irish Church in the decades immediately after the penal laws.

Never slow to see how a local situation could be turned to their own advantage, the British Empire builders lost no time in devising a scheme to win over the Catholic bishops and through them to keep all rebel tendencies among the oppressed Irish people under tight control. They invented Maynooth. For the modest outlay of £24,000 they offered in 1795 to erect and endow a seminary in Maynooth for the education of Irish Catholic priests. The Irish bishops accepted and allowed themselves to become 'the moral police force' for the British. As part of the arrangement, all the staff and students of the college were required to take an oath of allegiance to the British Crown in the following terms:

> I will be faithful and bear true allegiance to our most gracious sovereign, Lord King George III, and him will defend to the utmost of my power against all conspiracies and attempts whatever, that shall be made against his person, crown and dignity; and I will to my utmost endeavour to disclose and make known to His Majesty and heirs, all treasons and traitorous conspiracies which may be forced against him or them; and I do faithfully promise to maintain, support and defend to the utmost of my power, the succession of the crown in His Majesty's family against any person or persons whatever.

The oath was administered from the first year of the opening of the college up to the year of the Fenian rising in 1867 and was a big factor in the development of generations of Catholic clergy, strongly opposed to Irish Republicanism.

It was an investment which paid enormous dividends to the British and they lost no opportunity to call in the favours. Through the exercise of secret diplomacy in Rome

they were invariably able from time to time to have the Irish
bishops pressurised by the Vatican into doing whatever it
was they wanted them to do.

For example, in 1798, Monsignor Erskine in Rome urged
Archbishop Troy of Dublin to condemn the United Irishmen. Within days the bishops complied with a pastoral letter. Later in the year, priests in Wexford were described in
most scurrilous language by their superiors.

In 1800, the Catholic bishops and under their guidance,
most of the priests and 'Catholics of standing', enthusiastic-
ally supported the union. According to Lecky:

> The Catholic bishops appear to have been unanimous in fa-
> vour of the union. Archbishop Troy of Dublin was indefati-
> gable in procuring signatures to addresses ... the Archbishop
> of Cashel wrote to Archbishop Troy expressing his decided
> good wishes for the measure, and promising to exert his influ-
> ence 'discreetly' in the counties of Tipperary and Waterford to
> procure the signatures of respectable Catholics ... Dr Moylan,
> the Bishop of Cork, wrote 'The Roman Catholics in general are
> avowedly for the measure....'

In 1834, the hierarchy passed a resolution in response to
pressure from abroad requiring priests to steer clear of involvement in the controversy over tithes.

In 1844, again in response to British pressure, the Irish
Primate, Dr Crolly, was informed by the Vatican that the
Fransconi direction of 1839, requiring that the Irish bishops
refrain, 'not only from all political activity but from even all
semblance of political involvement', had been ignored. He
was reminded that ecclesiastics were in duty bound to
'separate themselves from all secular concerns [notably the
Repeal movement at that time], to inculcate subjection to the
temporal power [the British] in civil matters and to dissipate
popular excitements'. The Primate was further instructed to
admonish all ecclesiastics who defied that teaching.

The Fenian oath of allegiance to an Irish Republic 'now
virtually established' was obviously in direct conflict with
the Maynooth oath of allegiance to a foreign king whose
only title to Ireland was based on conquest of the country by

force. In view of the Church's continued acquiescence to the injustices and oppression of that foreign king, its condemnation of Fenian methods accordingly fell largely upon deaf ears.

The image of the Church had been damaged by its unholy alliance with the British Government for the sake of the paltry Maynooth donation. It appeared to have become the Church of the middle classes and a strong supporter of middle class values. As Dr Crolly, President of Maynooth, had pointed out, the diocesan clergy were:

> ... generally the sons of farmers who must be comfortable in order to meet the expenses, of tradesmen, shopkeepers and not a very small proportion of them are the children of opulent merchants and rich farmers and graziers ... the students overwhelmingly came from what in Ireland is considered the middling class.

Its record during the Famine years showed the extent to which the Maynooth oath had corrupted it. The bishops' pastorals proclaimed, as did Prime Ministers Sir Robert Peel and Lord John Russell, that the landlord must be paid his rent even if that involved selling corn and animals which could be used to keep the people alive; property rights transcended the rights of people dying of starvation; all authority, including that of the British came from a divine source; the Famine was the 'Will of God'. Even when one of their colleagues, Dr John Hughes, Archbishop of New York, warned them that they were blaspheming, 'in charging on the Almighty the result of human doings', that 'there is no law of Heaven – no law of nature – that forbids a starving man to seize on bread wherever he can find it', and that they should be careful 'not to blaspheme Providence by calling this God's Famine', the Irish Church as an institution felt it had more to get by bending the knee to the British than by standing up for the rights of the hungry. Alone among the hierarchy, Dr Maginn of Derry came out in their favour. In a letter to Lord Stanley he wrote, 'If the Irish priesthood have anything to answer for to God it is for the tameness and the silence and the patient submission with which most of them looked upon the wrongs and the ruin of their country'.

The depression and disillusionment in Ireland in the wake of the Famine, is hard to imagine today. In spite of the military fiasco of 1867 and the criticism of the 'wise men', the Fenians restored some morale in the people at a time when it could hardly have been lower. They proved that they were not afraid to face British guns at the height of British imperial power. They proved also that deep in the hearts of the common people – for the Fenian organisation was essentially an organisation of the common people – was a spirit of resentment to foreign rule which was only waiting to be tapped: it was this same spirit that subsequently was repeatedly tapped. They proved finally that they were neither ashamed nor repentant for what they had done. Even those leaders who were awarded long terms of imprisonment – O'Donovan Rossa for life, O'Leary, Luby, Devoy, Kickham and others for periods of up to twenty years, resumed their work in the movement after their release – many of them broken in health.

While the original leaders were out of commission, the Brotherhood was re-organised. New men came into it and a new constitution was framed which provided for a secret organisation, governed by a representative supreme council, democratically elected, to exercise the supreme authority formerly vested in the supreme head centre – James Stephens. Thus re-organised, the new body settled down to the long wait before another attempt could be made to undo the union by force. In the meantime, a small section of the membership split off to pursue an extreme policy of assassination and dynamiting.

It was claimed by some that Fenianism had a big influence on Gladstone's policies for the better government of Ireland – disestablishment of the church, land reform and so on. But these were never the aims of the Fenians. What they wanted was independence not reform. It was a test of their conviction and patience that they could keep a secret organisation of this sort alive in the midst of inactivity for a full fifty years, before a new generation – Clarke, MacDermott, Pearse, McDonagh, Ceannt and Plunkett – 'who had been re-baptised in the Fenian faith', could avail themselves of the opportunity presented by Britain's involvement in the First World War, and, in 1916, make a fresh bid for freedom.

5

'Don't tell it Joe'

The Invincibles

PART 1: 'Inner Circle' of the Land League?

Landlordism in Ireland was always a hell on earth for those who had to earn their living from agriculture. In the main, the lords and masters owned large tracts of land, granted to them for nothing or almost nothing by the Crown, following various wars and confiscations. As John Fitzgibbon put it, 'Confiscation is their common title'. As with most things received for nothing, it was wasted. Most of those who got it were unable to work all they got, and had to let large portions of it. They grossly exploited their tenants and gave no credit for improvements made by them. In fact, they did the opposite: rents tended to be increased for improvements effected.

The Famine had serious economic consequences for many landlords – rental income had fallen and local taxation (poor rates) had risen. Combined with their usual extravagance, this led a large number into serious debt. To meet the demands of creditors these were forced to sell parts of their estates under the new Encumbered Estates Act which provided ways for overcoming the elaborate machinery by which existing law guarded against alienation of estates. Buyers were generally rich townsmen, land jobbers and speculators, out to maximise profits from their investment. They bought from the landlords at the lowest price possible, at a time when the landlords were forced to sell, and then tried to squeeze the last penny out of the tenants.

Galtee Boy and Lord Leitrim

The treatment meted out to tenants by these speculators was often worse than that of the old landlords. One such adventurer was Nathaniel Buckley, a Liverpool businessman who bought some 21,000 acres of the Galtee mountains from James King, fifth Earl of Kingston, owner of the Kingston Estate near Mitchelstown. This was the same estate that was owned in 1766 by Robert King, the second Earl of Kingston, when the Whiteboys were active in his area. Buckley employed an agent named Patten Smith Bridge, whose ill-treatment of poor tenants on the barren slopes of the mountains was notorious. In 1876, an attempt was made to shoot him but the shot intended for him killed his jarvey instead. A man named Crowe was hanged for the offence.

John Sarsfield Casey, a local Fenian and frequent contributor to nationalist organs under the *nom de plume*, 'Galtee Boy', took up the case and wrote to the press giving full details of the rack-renting on the miserable mountainy holdings. Bridge sued for libel but the jury disagreed, which was tantamount to a victory for 'Galtee Boy', given that the law was entirely on the side of the landlord. In the course of the trial, tenants gave evidence of the appalling drudgery of having to bring lime, manure and other materials up the steep slopes of the Galtee mountains on the backs of men, women and children, to fertilise scrub land for which little or no rent had been paid previously, and of the unremitting toil required to meet the rents now demanded by Buckley. The 'Galtee Boy' trial gave much publicity to the widespread exploitation of the time, and to the laws which regarded the human tillers of the soil as merely part of the livestock to be worked to the utmost in the interests of the land owners.

Two years after the Mitchelstown shooting, Lord Leitrim

and two of his guards were assassinated while driving near Millford in county Donegal. It was considered by the people to be an act of retaliatory justice and nobody was ever brought to trial for the deed, although 'the whole country-side knew' who did it. Leitrim had not only the reputation of being a grinding landlord but he was also accused of exercising his power as a landlord to destroy the virtue of some of his tenants' daughters. His death was an act of revenge by a young man whose sister had been grievously wronged in this way. It was regarded as just reward for the infamous privilege, known in France as *droits des seigneurs*, a privilege which helped to precipitate the French Revolution and sent many a noble libertine to the guillotine.

The shootings on the Galtees and in Donegal were only two examples from the times, but the British Government remained unconcerned at the plight of the people who had to endure the conditions which gave rise to such events. Their answer to violence and social unrest of every kind was not to find out the cause of the trouble but to apply sufficient coercion and military force to repress it. Regardless of whether the Government in power was Tory or Liberal, policy towards Ireland was always the same. During the second half of the 1870s, Disraeli's Tory Government was in power and the Chief Secretary for Ireland was the inimitable James Lowther. Lowther had nothing but contempt for Ireland, and everything Irish, and never made the slightest attempt to conceal either in Dublin Castle or in Parliament his detestation of the inferior race of beings for which he now had been given some responsibility. Unburdened by any noticeable intellectual gifts, his chief interest appeared to be in the turf, where he was familiarly known as 'Jimmy' Lowther. His approach to the explosive situation building up in the country under his administration was to bury his head in the sand and persistently deny that there was anything wrong. By the end of his term in 1880, prices had hit rock bottom, the people were unable to pay the rack-rents demanded, famine was threatened, the country was in turmoil and the organisation set up by Davitt to protect the interests of the oppressed tenantry – The Land League – was spreading rapidly.

Buckshot Forster and suppression of the Land League

Lowther's successor as Chief Secretary, in the Liberal Government which followed the general election of 1880, was William E. Forster. Nominally a Liberal, but every bit as much a British imperialist as his Tory predecessor, Forster continued with the same repressive policies and shortly earned for himself the unenviable nickname of 'Buckshot Forster'. Coercion measures of all sorts were vigorously enforced. Leading members of Parliament were prosecuted for conspiracy. Michael Davitt, chief organiser of the Land League, had his ticket of leave cancelled and was returned to prison. In March 1881 a new Coercion Act became law. Habeas corpus was suspended. Hundreds of respectable men, merchants, farmers and professional people were thrown into jail for indefinite periods, on mere suspicion of being supporters of the Land League. There was not even the usual mockery of a trial – no charge, no accusation or accusers. Women and even children were regularly charged with most ridiculous offences. On 13 October 1881, Parnell was arrested and imprisoned in Kilmainham. A week later, on 20 October, the Land League was suppressed and Forster proclaimed from his command post in Dublin Castle:

> Now we hereby warn all persons that the said association, styling itself the Irish Land League or whatsoever other name it may be called or known, is an unlawful and criminal association ... and we do hereby call on all loyal and well-affected subjects of the Crown to aid us in upholding and maintaining the authority of the law and the supremacy of the queen in this her realm in Ireland.

Murders at Belmullet

In the same month, a British officer, acting on his orders to strike terror in the people, ordered that a volley of buckshot be fired into a crowd of women and children gathering for a meeting at Grawhill near Belmullet and then that they be charged with bayonets. Mrs Mary Deane, a widowed mother, was shot dead by the buckshot and Ellen McDonagh, a young girl, was stabbed to death in the bayonet charge. Nobody was ever brought to justice for the crime. Commenting on these murders, Mr Joseph Cowen of the *Newcastle Chronicle*, himself a Liberal, wrote:

> If Ireland had been Bulgaria, Montenegro, or Greece, the language used, and the feelings expressed, would have nothing in common with what is now in vogue. Nothing can surpass the withering sarcasm which Continental politicians of every class cast upon this new phase of 'nationality interest', as they call it, developed in Her Majesty's Government. The men that have so often stood before Europe as the friends of every slave shivering in his chains, are now themselves putting in force as remorseless a despotism as is operating in Moscow.

The Land League's Response

It was against this background that the Irish Invincibles sprang into being. According to P.J. Tynan, described as 'Number One' in his own account of the organisation, the Invincibles were recruited from the inner circle of the Land League when it became obvious that Gladstone and Forster were determined to crush the League by force. In October 1881, this certainly appeared to be the intention. Up to half a million people had already joined the League, but Davitt and the principal leaders were in jail and the organisation itself was declared illegal. Some members still at large, however, joined the Invincibles. Were it not for the Parnellites, Tynan maintained, there would have been no Invincibles.

Parnell's Attitude to Secret Physical Resistance

It would appear from a report published in the *New York Herald* of 2 January 1880, long before the severe repressive measures of 1881 were introduced, that Parnell supported a secret physical force movement in certain circumstances. 'A true revolutionary movement in Ireland,' he is reported as saying, 'should, in my opinion, partake of both a constitutional and an illegal character. It should be both an open and a secret organisation, using the constitution for its own purposes, but also taking advantage of its secret combination'. At a banquet in Cork during the election of 1880, Joseph Biggar declared, with the apparent approval of Parnell and all other senior Irish Parliamentary Party members present on that occasion, that if the constitutional course they were pursuing at that juncture failed in its objects, he thought Ireland might be able to produce another Hartmann (Russian revolutionary) 'and probably with better results'.

The Mysterious Invincible Executive

Tynan states that at about this time he himself was approached,

> ... and asked to join the new movement ... from his early association with the IRB ... he felt satisfied that the party of action had some new movement in preparation which would speedily develop ... To be approached by a prominent and trusted Parnellite official to join an active movement of the most extreme kind in the very chamber where Parliamentary members sat to consult and arrange 'Legal and Constitutional Agitation' staggered and astonished him. He felt ... as if a veil had fallen from his eyes, and that the policy of shaming the invader out of Ireland was only a huge sham; that physical resistance to tyranny was the under-current of this gigantic movement.

He promised to give his answer next day. Overnight he consulted with an old Nationalist friend and told him of the interview in the Parnellite chambers. His friend gave him 'a detailed history of the National undertaking, which was the creation of those who held the Irish reins of office', and told him that he himself was already 'a member of the new Invincible administration'. Next day, he was enrolled as an Invincible. 'There,' he says, 'in the Parnellite Parliamentary chamber, the temple of "legal agitation", he received and accepted (not for the first time) the obligation of an Irish revolutionary soldier'. Before he left, he was asked to initiate another new member into the organisation, and there in the same chamber where he was himself initiated, he repeated the ceremony to a new recruit, 'a gentleman of social standing, good means and highly honourable reputation, a prominent Parnellite, and to the outer world a firm believer in "moral persuasion"'.

The Dublin Invincibles

He states that he was sent to Dublin shortly afterwards to take supreme command of the Invincibles there. At the time, they were apparently organised into what was called the Dublin Council, 'composed of four men, each of whom controlled a number of sub-officers, and these again had under their immediate command the rank and file of the organisation'. 'The Dublin Invincibles,' he continues, 'were almost altogether composed of IRB men, either from members already enrolled, or ex-members ... In country districts, the Invincibles were principally composed of ... members of the suppressed Land League'. He named John Walsh, an ex-Land League organiser, as the man who organised Dublin before his own arrival. Walsh went to America and died of paralysis in Bellvue Hospital New York in 1894. Among the organisers in the country districts he named P.J. Sheridan, described as 'a true and tried Irish Nationalist, although a prominent Parnellite'. He states that Sheridan was also an active member of the Land League and an elected member of the first executive council of the League. It appears that Sheridan also died in America, following an accident in 1892, in which he was crushed between a vehicle and a gate in his ranch, eight miles south of Monte Vista, Colorado.

In addition to the foregoing, Tynan mentions Mr and Mrs Frank Byrne who lived at 4 Gothic Villas, Avondale Road, near the Peckham Rye railway station in London, as principal figures behind the organisation of the Dublin Invincibles. Frank Byrne was secretary to Parnell and, according to informer Carey, he was also secretary to the 'Constitutional organisation' in Great Britain, and a Fenian.

He had earlier served with distinction in the Franco-Prussian war, and had received several decorations. He was an officer in the *Compagnie Irlandaise*, which fought under General Bourbaki in the army of the east, and was wounded at the battle of Montbéliard. During the trials of the Invincibles in 1883, he escaped to France, and the French Government refused a demand for his extradition, partly, he himself maintained, because of his service in the French army. Following his release in France he went immediately to America and arrived in New York with his wife and children on 4 April 1883. He remained active in Irish national societies in America for the next eleven years, and at the time of his death in February 1894, was a member of Division 12 of the local branch of the Hibernians in Providence.

'Byrne's wife,' according to a report published in *Providence Journal*, 17 February 1894, 'was as ardent a patriot as himself, and she partook fully of his ideas. Her sympathy, it is said, was not of the passive kind, but she was also an active member of the secret Irish societies. It was the knowledge of her activity that led the English Government to apprehend her as well as her husband'. She is credited with being the woman who brought to Dublin the surgical knives with which the Phoenix Park assassinations were committed. These were said to have been lying for days in a drawer in the London offices of the Irish National League in the headquarters of the Irish Parliamentary Party in Westminster Chambers, almost within reach of one of their future victims, Lord Frederick Cavendish, when he was sitting in the chamber. Mrs Byrne was descended from an old Scottish family. Born in Haddington Road, Dublin, on 29 September 1854, she was the second daughter of Arthur Moneypenny and Frances Kelly, and a direct descendant of Lord Moneypenny of Scotland.

Patrick Joseph Percy Tynan, the mysterious 'Number One'

In an account written by his friend and companion, Patrick Kinsella, former station master at Blackrock, Co. Dublin, and published in the American edition of Tynan's book, it is stated that Tynan was commanding officer of the military Invincibles in Dublin city but that this military body was different from the civilian organisation which sprang into existence all over the country after the suppression of the Land League. The names of the leaders of the civilian organisation were never made known publicly, he adds.

The Times of 4 March 1883 states, however: 'It is a mistake ... to suppose that because of his title he [Tynan] is a person of commanding authority in the conspiracy. He was not the leader or head of the "Invincibles" but an organiser having higher rank than other agents, but still subordinate to a superior executive'. The report adds: 'He was in Dublin not long ago, but managed to get away before Carey gave information about him. He is an Irishman and lived in Kingston for some time, where his wife had a lodging house. He afterwards removed to London, which appears to have been his headquarters'. According to *The Irish Times* of 16 April 1883, he 'lived in London at 4 Merrow Villas, Avondale Road, Peckham Rye, just six doors from Frank Byrne, with whose family he was on terms of great intimacy'.

Kinsella goes on to say that Tynan was a frequent visitor to the Land League headquarters in Palace Chambers, Westminster, and took a prominent part in all meetings and discussions during the winter of 1881; that he spoke from the same carriage as William Redmond in Hyde Park, protesting at the arrest of Parnell; that he was intimately associated with several of the officials in the Irish Office in London; that he was a frequent visitor to these Government offices at Queen Anne's Gate; and that he was personally friendly with the officials who travelled around with Mr Forster and other Irish Secretaries.

During the preliminary examination of suspects arrested in connection with the Phoenix Park assassinations, Carey gave to the police a description of Tynan. He said he knew him very well, both by appearance and having had personal relations with him, but he had no name for him and knew nothing more about him. He described him as a gentlemanly person, who he felt certain was, or had been, a military man.

The few Invincibles in Dublin with whom he had personal relations knew him by no other name than Number One. All sorts of guesses were made as to who he might be and eventually it became such a mystery that it began to be said that Number One was only a fictional creation of Carey.

When the trials of those charged with the assassinations opened on 9 April 1883, the authorities had apparently established, or thought they had established, that the principal figure in charge of the conspiracy, known as Number One, had been staying in Jury's Hotel, Dublin, for some time prior to Saturday, 6 May 1882, and that he had left Dublin on the Thursday evening after the event. They felt certain they had a clue to his current whereabouts, and that they would soon succeed in capturing him. The Crown counsel went so far as to say that he would for certain have Number One in the dock by the following Saturday. On Monday, 16 April, however, *The Irish Times* reported that P.J. Tynan, the notorious Number One, had already made good his escape to America but that detectives in London were continuing their enquiries in regard to him.

Apparently, the previous day, the London police had entered Frank Byrne's house in Avondale Road, and found in an album there, a photograph which matched Carey's description of the mysterious Number One' 'But for the finding of this photograph,' says Kinsella, 'Number One would have remained, like the Invincible Executive, the greatest mystery of the nineteenth century'. Follow-up enquiries revealed that Tynan had joined the thirteenth Middlesex Volunteers early in 1882, had become, and was still, a member of Company 1, Queen's Westminsters, a very special London Volunteer Regiment commanded by the Duke of Westminster. It also came to light that on Easter Monday, just weeks before 6 May 1882, he was with his regiment and shared in the sham battle of Portsmouth. He also attended the annual muster of the 'Queen's' in Hyde Park. Most startling of all was his part in the pageant which took place early in December 1882, seven months after the assassinations in the Phoenix Park and one month before the Dublin arrests, 'when the new Law Courts in the Strand, London were officially opened by the queen in royal state'. On this occasion Tynan was selected as a member of the Queen's Westminsters to share with Her Majesty's household troops, the Life and Horse Guards, the distinction of forming part of Her Majesty's Guard of Honour.

'There are few things more romantic in history,' commented Kinsella, 'than the queen's guards saluting the captain of a body of Irish guerrilla soldiers engaged in a species of terrible warfare, against what these Irishmen believed were their country's bitter enemies'. According to the report in *The Irish Times*: 'The object of a conspirator in allying himself with a volunteer corps is the subject of various conjectures. Whether it was to serve as a blind to his other movements or to obtain military training is unknown'. Tynan lived for many years after 1883 in America with his wife and eight children, but does not appear ever to have commented on this aspect of his career.

Attorney General's Statement

In his statement to the jury at the 1883 trials, the Irish attorney general stated that the Invincible organisation was formed in Dublin in the autumn of 1881 for the stated purpose of assassinating top officials of the British Government. 'The plan was,' he said, 'that it should consist of members not exceeding fifty – I believe ... it does not appear that there were ever more than thirty ... who should be under the control of four heads, who might be described as a sort of committee of action in Dublin ... The first four persons, who were the committee and established this organisation in Dublin were ... James Mullet, Edward McCaffrey, Daniel Curley and James Carey. The Invincible organisation was not a Fenian organisation so far as we know, but the members of it were persons who were selected from that body'. He names the organisers as Edward McCaffrey, John Walsh and a person in a superior position known only by the name of Number One. He stated that funds were supplied from abroad and that a man named Sheridan, travelling incognito as Fr Murphy, arranged for the supply of arms including daggers and surgical knives.

In the autumn of 1881 the turmoil in Ireland had reached boiling point. The Land League was suppressed, habeas corpus was suspended, Parnell and other leaders were in Kilmainham and hundreds of ordinary people were held in jail without trial. Tynan's account states that the leading figures in the Invincible movement met and decided that, although a war to secure the independence of the country was not feasible so soon after the failed Fenian rising, some direct physical retaliation should be attempted in response to the suppression of the Land League. He continues: 'By the earliest council held by the Executive of the Invincibles it was resolved that ... the offices of "Chief Secretary" and "Under-Secretary of State" ... should be kept vacant by the continued "suppression" of their holders and that a final council of war in a small foreign town commissioned three men to take charge of the conduct of affairs ... All of the Invincible Executive,' he adds, 'were high Parnellite officials'.

Forster's Many Escapes

During the following months, several attempts were made to assassinate Chief Secretary Forster pursuant to these orders. Tynan gives details of some of them. On one occasion the Invincibles had news that Forster would leave his residence in the Phoenix Park at 11 o'clock on a certain date. It was decided to attack his carriage at the corner of John Street and Ellis Quay near the park where the street narrows. The plan was that the Invincibles would have a car near the Chief Secretary's lodge which would follow in the wake of Forster's carriage, and that James Carey would sit beside the driver to signal his arrival to the first Invincible sentry, whose duty it was to take up the signal and pass it along the line to those in position to carry out the killing at the appointed spot. At a final planning meeting the night before the intended attack, Carey begged to be relieved of the dangerous duty of occupying the box seat of the vehicle following Forster's carriage, pleading his large family. The change in plan was not, however, notified to the first sentry on the ground, who, expecting to see Carey on one of the vehicles coming down the road and to receive a message from him, failed to signal Forster's approach. As a result, Forster's carriage passed through unscathed.

On another occasion, arrangements were made to meet him off a certain train in Westland Row but by another chapter of accidents he escaped. On a third occasion, it was again arranged to ambush him at the spot on the quays where the first abortive attempt was made. This time the Invincibles' vehicle was to precede the Chief Secretary's carriage. When the official carriage arrived at the appointed spot it was discovered that there were ladies travelling along with Forster, and the attack was called off.

A final attempt was made when Forster was leaving for London at the end of April 1882. It was planned to stop his carriage at St Mark's church, Brunswick Street (now Pearse Street). Men were put in position to carry out the attack, but when the official carriage arrived with Forster's family it was discovered that Forster himself was not with them. The Invincibles waited around in the rain, sheltering in doorways, until 11.45 p.m. the departure time for the last mail train from Westland Row, unaware that their target had once again evaded them, having stolen out of the Castle early in the afternoon and driven to Dún Laoghaire (then Kingston) instead of going by train.

On Thursday, 4 May, news broke of Forster's resignation in protest at the Kilmainham Treaty. Number One asked for instructions from the Invincible Executive in the new situation. The previous evening, he had already instructed the chief of the Dublin Council to have his men ready by Friday for an attack on the Under Secretary. On Friday morning, he received a reply from the Executive informing him that nothing was in any way changed, that action was to continue, that he was to remain on the ground and on no account to leave Dublin. When he arrived at the

Phoenix Park on Friday, he met the Invincible officer in charge at the entrance gate. The rest of his group were reconnoitring the area inside with a view to learning something about the Under Secretary's movements. Number One advised that unless action could be taken at once, it had better be postponed. He then arranged to meet this section later that evening to discuss plans for the following day.

Murder of Children in Ballina

While the meeting was in progress, news arrived of an unprovoked attack with buckshot and bayonet by the police on a band of young boys and girls – mostly children under twelve – parading in Ballina with tin whistles and drums to celebrate Parnell's release from custody. One of them, Patrick Melody, aged twelve, was stabbed to death, and many others were seriously wounded. It was the kind of news with which Ireland was familiar under Forster's administration and which served only to harden the determination of those in the physical resistance movement.

PART 2: Phoenix Park Assassinations

Having failed in their many attempts to assassinate Forster, the Invincibles now decided to move swiftly ahead with their efforts to assassinate the permanent Under Secretary, T.H. Burke, instead. Thomas Henry Burke was an Irishman and a Catholic. He was an unflinching supporter of the British connection, dedicated to keeping Ireland bound hand and foot to the Union Jack. He was regarded as the evil adviser in Forster's coercionist administration, an employer of informers, an advocate of imprisonment without trial and all the other draconian measures designed to break the spirit of resistance in the people. Two attempts were made to meet up with him on Friday, 5 May, but neither succeeded. Mr Burke failed to turn up. Two separate attempts were also planned for the following day, Saturday, 6 May. The second of these succeeded. Mr Burke and the new Chief Secretary for Ireland, Lord Frederick Cavendish, were assassinated in the Phoenix Park at about 7.17 that evening.

Almost twelve months later, over twenty Invincibles were charged with murder and conspiracy to murder. Five of the accused – Brady, Kelly, Fagan, Caffrey and Curley – were condemned to death, and were hanged in Kilmainham. Three were given life sentences and others were sentenced to various terms of imprisonment. All were convicted mainly on the evidence of four colleagues, who turned informer: James Carey; Michael Kavanagh – the driver of a side car used by the attackers; Joseph Smith – a labourer in the Board of Works who worked in the Lower Castle Yard; and Robert Farrell – a member of the Fenian Brotherhood who knew Dan Curley to be a member of the inner circle of the Invincibles. The story of what took place that day is based almost entirely on the evidence of these informers and on the account by P.J. Tynan.

According to Carey, he went to Kingsbridge, beside the Phoenix Park, around 10.30 that morning in a cab driven by Fitzharris, in accordance with arrangements made the previous evening with Number One. Lord Frederick Cavendish had arrived in Dún Laoghaire that morning also, to take up his post as Chief Secretary and was accompanied by the new Viceroy, John Poyntz, Earl Spencer. As permanent Under Secretary for Ireland, Burke was involved with the formalities of inducting the new arrivals to their appointments, and apparently had gone to his work in the Castle early that morning. It was unlikely that he would leave the Castle again until late in the evening. The projected morning attack had, therefore, to be abandoned. Number One accordingly left the park area and was not involved in the attack which took place later that day. Carey went on to Andrew Wrenn's public house in Dame Street where he met Joe Brady, Kelly and others. Wrenn's pub was directly opposite the entrance gate to the Lower Castle Yard and was widely used by the Invincibles as a rendezvous.

Michael Kavanagh, the driver of the side car used by the attackers that day, gave an account of the morning's activities from the Dame Street end. He was engaged for the day by Tim Kelly; then he went to Anne Street where he picked up Brady at about 9.45; next he drove to the corner where he picked up two more – Patrick Delaney and Tom Caffrey – and drove all four to Fishamble Street. He went into Wrenn's pub with them and had a drink there. Later, he met another man there, named Mattley, and had a drink with him also, not at Wrenn's, but in the public house above it, nearer to Parliament Street. After his drink he came out to his horse outside Wrenn's, and waited. Some time later, Tim Kelly came out. He drove Kelly to Thomas Street and back to Wrenn's again. Next he drove Kelly to Thomas Street a second time and back to the pub once more. On his return the second time he met Brady outside the pub door. Brady told him to pull in at the opposite side of the street, beside the Munster and Leinster Bank, and wait until the procession had passed. When it had passed, Brady beckoned him from the other side to take his car to the corner of Sycamore Alley (now Sycamore Street) and wait there – which he did.

None of the Invincibles was acquainted with Burke's appearance, but Carey had met a man in the park the previous day – 5 May – named Joseph Smith, who was employed by the Board of Works in the Lower Castle Yard and who knew Burke to see. Smith had been a Fenian, and Carey there and then enrolled him as an Invincible, in the presence of 'Number One' and Tim Kelly. Smith came off work about 3 o'clock that Saturday, and was met by Carey, who accompanied him to Wrenn's pub.

During the afternoon of 6 May, therefore, seven Invincibles – Joe Brady, Timothy Kelly, Tom Caffrey, Patrick Delaney, James Carey, Joseph Hanlon and Joseph Smith – had rendezvoused at Wrenn's in preparation for an attack on Burke in the park, when he would be returning home after his work. At about 4.50 they left the pub and set off in two parties. Carey, Smith and Hanlon went to the cab owned by James Fitzharris which was waiting at the corner of Parliament Street and Essex Street. Brady, Kelly, Caffrey, and Delaney boarded the sidecar owned by Michael Kavanagh which had been waiting only yards away at Sycamore Alley. The cab was understood to have left first, although it does not appear to have arrived first in the park. It was driven along the quays in the direction of Kingsbridge, crossed the river at Kingsbridge, went straight through the main gates of the Phoenix Park and up the main road until it came to a point opposite the polo grounds, where it halted. The occupants got out – Carey and Smith crossed to the right hand side of the road to watch a polo match; Hanlon remained on the left hand side, watching a game of cricket.

The sidecar left Sycamore Alley almost immediately after the cab. It proceeded along the same route as that taken by the cab until it crossed the river at Kingsbridge. Instead of proceeding through the main entrance gates of the Phoenix Park as the cab had done, however, it went along Conyngham Road and entered the park via the first gate on the right (the Islandbridge gate). It then went diagonally through the park until it came to the Chief Secretary's residence (now the Papal Nuncio's residence), around the Phoenix (which stood in the middle of the road), and down the main road in the direction of the city, in the expectation of meeting Fitzharris' cab coming up in the opposite direction.

The cab had not yet arrived, however, and Brady ordered Kavanagh to reverse his car and take his four passengers back up the main road – again towards the Phoenix – to a point on the left hand side going up, opposite the Viceregal Lodge, some 1,400 yards from the Gough monument and 600 yards from the Phoenix, where it was planned to make the attack on Burke. He then sent Kavanagh down once more to the vicinity of the Gough monument with an empty car, and instructions to wait there until he got further orders. While Kavanagh was doing this shuttle trip, Fitzharris had actually arrived in the vicinity of the city end of the polo ground some 300 yards up from the Gough monument.

Curley and Fagan had also arrived in the polo ground/ Gough area at around the same time. Curley came over to the polo ground when he saw Carey there, and Carey records his conversation with him: 'Curley said, "What are you doing here?" I replied, "I am looking at this game. I never saw it before." He said, "It's not here you should be, you should be over; you can't tell the moment he might be coming up."'

Curley didn't want any slip up this time. After Curley's reprimand, Carey took up his position on the bench beside Smith some 300 yards from the Gough monument and about 1,100 yards from the projected assassination position. Curley pointed out again that signalling Burke's arrival could be better done from the car than the cab, and he accordingly ordered Kavanagh to take his vehicle to the other side – the left going up – and have the horse facing towards the Phoenix monument. He then departed in Fitzharris' cab, taking Fagan and Hanlon with him, and joined the main party at the ambush position opposite the Viceregal Lodge. The cab turned around some time later and remained on the Viceregal Lodge side of the road, facing towards the city, until after the ambush.

The cab and car waited in these positions, along the

main road, for about an hour and half before anything happened. Then at about 7 o'clock or a little earlier, Lord Frederick Cavendish entered the park on foot, on his way to the
Chief Secretary's residence opposite the Phoenix, having apparently walked unaccompanied from his office in the
Castle. When he had passed the Gough monument, another
man, who turned out to be Mr Burke, the permanent Under
Secretary, was seen to alight from a passing car and join
him. Both were seen to walk on together. It was alleged
afterwards that it was an arranged meeting for the purpose
of discussing the sensitive question of security for the Chief
Secretary himself.

Kavanagh saw the two men approach along the footpath. One of them was dressed in grey and the other in
black. Carey and Smith (the man who had been sitting with
him on a bench at the polo pitch side of the road) saw them
also, and came running across the road. They told him to
look sharp. Smith said that when he saw Mr Burke coming
up the footpath he cried out, 'It is very like Mr Burke ... It is
Mr Burke ... Well up with you on the car', and the two
boarded the car. The horse was feeding at the time and Kavanagh took off the nosebag. Kavanagh got very nervous
and very white. As they were being driven up the road,
Smith saw Carey take out a white handkerchief. Kavanagh
drove towards the Phoenix as fast as he could go, passing
Fitzharris' cab, which was stationary, as he went. He also
saw Carey take out a white handkerchief and put it to his
mouth. Carey gave it a shake, in the act of wiping his nose.
Carey and Smith got down when he came up to where the
main group was waiting, opposite the Viceregal Lodge. He
remained on the car. Either Carey or Smith said, 'Mind, it's
the big man'. He saw Brady, Kelly and Caffrey in the main
group. There were others there also whom he did not know.
One of the group told him to go up further.

Carey himself said he told the group, 'Look, the man in
the grey suit'. He asked Brady what was he do with Smith,
and Brady replied, 'Tell him to go off to hell out of that'.
Smith then left the scene in the direction of the Chapelizod

(now St Mary's) gate. After Smith had gone, Carey asked what was he himself to do and was told he was no longer wanted. He accordingly went diagonally across the green and through a grove, in the direction of the Islandbridge gate (the gate through which Kavanagh had driven his car about two hours previously). As he went, he saw Mr Burke and a companion coming along the footpath. His colleagues, who were on the same footpath – directly opposite the Viceregal Lodge – now appeared to have formed themselves into three groups, some twelve feet or thereabouts apart. The first group consisted of Curley, Fagan and Hanlon, the second of Brady and Kelly, and the third of Caffrey and Delaney. All were facing down towards the city. From Carey's position, which was about 250 yards away, Burke and his companion appeared at first to have passed through the entire party. Then it appeared that the last two groups, namely Brady, Kelly, Caffrey and Delaney, turned sharply around so that Brady and Kelly were now closest to the victims. He saw Brady coming up to the gentleman in the grey suit until there was no space at all between them. He saw the motion of his left hand which was elevated at the time and then he saw no more. It was 7.17p.m.

Within about three minutes, the whole affair was over, and all seven of the attackers had disappeared from the scene, leaving two bodies on the ground behind them. Burke lay on the grass margin beside the footpath, and Cavendish lay on the roadway. Curley, Fagan and Hanlon got into the cab and Fitzharris drove off with them as fast as he could go, down the main road as far as the Gough monument, around to the left and out the North Circular gate, thus avoiding the Constabulary Depot, and vanished into the north city traffic. Brady, Kelly, Caffrey and Delaney (the same party that had come with Kavanagh from Wrenn's pub two hours previously) boarded his car and were driven at a furious pace out through the Chapelizod gate, into the village of Chapelizod, around to the left and up the steep hill to where the road passes under the railway line. There, they turned to the right and after a long detour through open country came to

Roundtown, and then on to Palmerston Road, Rathmines, where Kelly jumped off the car and took the tram into town. Kavanagh said that Brady and Caffrey also got off, somewhere along the route, because Brady wanted to wash his hands before he went into town. While he was washing, he told Kavanagh, to 'Listen if he could hear any noise'. Kavanagh also said that he gave Caffrey the white hat he himself was wearing in the park and took Caffrey's brown hat – which was too big for him – in exchange. The party then got on the car again and remained aboard until it reached Davy's public house in Leeson Street where they had a drink together and where Brady paid him £1 as portion of his hire for the day. Then the group dispersed. Thus, by 7.30, everybody involved in this operation was out of the park, and by 8.30, all were back again among the general population.

Carey said he met Joe Smith in the hollow of the Magazine on his way out of the park and that they both left together via the Islandbridge gate. He went into Cody's of Kilmainham. Smith and himself then came into town on the tram. He got off at College Green and went into Cleary's pub in Grafton Street. Cleary was an old friend of his. It was 8.07 when he arrived there. He remained in Cleary's for about half an hour. Curley called to his home at 8.30 but he was not at home. He met him later at about 9 o'clock at the corner of Holles Street.

He met Brady near his own house about 10 o'clock that night, and asked him if it was true that it was Lord Frederick Cavendish that was along with Burke. He had obviously learned this from his conversation with Curley an hour earlier. Brady said he did not know who it was, '... but only for himself [Cavendish] he wouldn't be the way he is'. Brady then gave his own account of what happened.

He said that first he let Burke pass by and then turned around and walked behind him. He overtook him and laid his left hand on his (Burke's) shoulder and stabbed him with the knife. While doing so, the other gentleman in black attacked him in the face with his umbrella and called him a ruffian. Had he not been thus annoyed, Brady said, Cavendish would have escaped; Cavendish ran out on the road after that and he (Brady) followed him and finished him there. When he looked around, he saw Kelly at Mr Burke and went back and finished him. He cut his throat. Carey asked him if it was true what he had heard, that when the thing was done, he was so cool as to wipe the knife on the grass, and Brady said, 'Yes'. He also told him about the detour they made after leaving the park and about washing the knives.

Kavanagh said that he met Brady again next morning, 7 May, when he came to his lodging house at Townsend Street. He came over to the stables and took him (Kavanagh) down under the arches where he gave £2 more. Afterwards he bought him some new harness. When he was paid, Kavanagh got his car repainted and put his mare out to grass. That evening, Carey met Brady again, along with Curley and Caffrey, at the house of Edward Caffrey at Peter Street where a full account of the affair was given to Number One.

Dramatis Personae

Patrick Joseph Percy Tynan, otherwise known as Number One, wrote an extensive account of the organisation. His book, *The Irish National Invincibles and Their Times*, was published in 1894. Though hotly pursued by the police at the time of the Phoenix Park trials in 1883, Tynan evaded capture and escaped to America with his wife and eight children. The information available about those involved in this dramatic event is derived from his book.

In the court records, Joe Brady is stated to have been twenty-six years old. His friend, Patrick Kinsella, the Blackrock station master, left this description of him:

> His step was light, buoyant and firm, his small and perfectly formed feet appearing to grasp the ground with the tenacity of the human hand. His mien was erect and graceful, giving him the appearance of a greater height than he possessed, while it neutralised or seemed to lessen his massive proportions ... He carried his head well but not stiffly thrown back ... His well shaped mouth was furnished with a perfect set of white teeth,

which glistened when he smiled that quiet smile which denotes and begets confidence; and his brown eyes were soft, expressive and unfathomable.

Timothy Kelly was not yet twenty-one years old. When evidence as to character was being given at his trial, Judge Peter O'Brien sarcastically exclaimed, 'Respectable! Of course he is respectable. They are all honourable and respectable men!' On the day of his execution, 9 June, he asked to be allowed spend his last hours in the cell from which his friend, Joe Brady, had walked to the scaffold on 14 May.

Daniel Curley was a married man, about thirty-two years old, of retiring disposition, slightly built, with dark curly hair, full beard and moustache. He was a master carpenter, who executed small contracts in Dublin City and suburbs. He was also a skilled mechanic. According to Patrick Kinsella who knew him well, 'His face bore a thoughtful cast which became animated and pleasing when in friendly company'. He was regarded as a very intelligent man with a strong will-power. He addressed the court before sentence of death was pronounced, saying he loved his country and was ready to suffer for her. As he left the dock, he cried out, 'God Save Ireland'.

Michael Fagan told the court before he was sentenced to death that he was a Fenian – in other words, an Irish revolutionary – and he would die one.

Thomas Caffrey was induced to plead guilty, and was also sentenced to death.

Lawrence Hanlon called out to the court before being sentenced to penal servitude for life, 'I will not be the last', meaning that for as long as the Union Jack flew over Ireland, there would be conspiracies, killings and hangings.

Joseph Mullet refused to recognise the court and was also sentenced to penal servitude for life. He was regarded as a very bright young man, above average in education, and told the court that there were other men who would remember and avenge him.

James Fitzharris, otherwise known as 'Skin-the-Goat', because of his habit of wearing a goatskin over his knees for protection while driving his cab, was a Fenian who kept faith with his Invincible oath to the end. He was found guilty of conspiracy, and imprisoned in Portlaoise for sixteen years.

Mrs Brady, mother of Joe Brady, stands out as a woman of exceptional character. She was deeply angered at the slander being circulated by the police about the supposed eagerness of members of the organisation to supply information that would lead to future captures and convictions. When she was taking leave of her son the day before his execution, she cried out through her grief, 'Joe, if you know anything don't tell it; bring your secret to the grave'.

Mrs Byrne, wife of Frank Byrne and direct descendant of Lord Moneypenny of Scotland, is credited with being the bearer from England of the surgical knives used in the Phoenix Park. Along with her husband, Frank, she got away to America before the trials started.

By public proclamation posted up on 8 May 1882, two days after the Phoenix Park assassinations, a reward of £10,000 sterling, equivalent to over £1 million today, was offered by the Viceroy, Lord Spencer, to 'anyone who will give such information as will lead to the arrest and conviction of the perpetrator or perpetrators of this murder and also the further reward of £5,000 is hereby offered to anyone who will give private information, and a free pardon is guaranteed to any such informant other than the actual perpetrators of the crime'. All of those involved were merely working men, and despite this very tempting inducement, the reward was never claimed. It says much for their integrity that none of them ever sought or would accept blood money. Even the four who did give information, while in custody, were trapped into doing so by the police, believing the police stories that their own colleagues, and in Carey's case, his own wife, were already informing against them. They received no financial reward.

Carey was a bricklayer by trade and a small builder. He was forty-five years old, with a large family, and appears to have been under constant pressure from his wife because of his membership of the Invincibles. He was shot on 29 July 1883 aboard the *Melrose* on his way to Natal while under police protection. His killer, Patrick O'Donnell – an Irish American – was executed in London on 18 December 1883. O'Donnell maintained that he was going to South Africa as a miner in search of work and that he was never commissioned directly or indirectly by the Invincibles or anyone else to pursue Carey. His story was that he met him on the way and, 'When I learned who he was, I resolved to pick a quarrel with him, to give him a chance of defending himself, and to shoot him if I could. I did so, and I don't regret it'.

Reaction of the Press

The daring character of the Phoenix Park attack stunned the Establishment and the world press. Two of the most senior members of the colonial power had been assassinated in broad daylight in what was described as 'the very heart and core of their stronghold', directly opposite the Viceregal Lodge, the official residence of the Lord Deputy, Representative of Her Majesty the queen, and surrounded by three military barracks (now Collins, Clancy and McKee), the headquarters of the constabulary and any number of detectives. The attackers were well aware of the risk involved in attempting assassination in such circumstances, and of the consequences for themselves should their plans go wrong. *The Times* wrote:

> The crime was not only brutal, but defiant and insolent. No one who has not actually examined the surroundings of the scene can be adequately impressed with this fact. All Dublin and many others examined the locality, and they see plainly what it all means – that the secret societies have challenged the whole power of the Executive, the Lord Lieutenant, the constabulary, and the military, in the very heart and core of their stronghold....

There was widespread support from Continental journals. *La Marseillaise* commented:

Thus it is no longer at simple landed proprietors that the musket balls of Ireland are aimed. They strike down the queen's delegates, in broad daylight. We pity the victims, but the immense pity we feel for the horrible situation of the Irish people, forbids us to show too much sympathy. Ireland, since the first day of the conquest, has been in a state of legitimate self defence. If at the cost of a series of outrages, she succeeds in casting off the terrible yoke which the sister island imposes on her, what friend of humanity would think of blaming her for it?

La Bastille wrote:

By executing Cavendish and Burke the unhappy slaves of English land law publicly declare that pseudo-liberal measures cannot satisfy them; ... that they have a goal in view, with a firm resolution of reaching it – namely, Irish independence.

Le Mot d'Ordre said:

We hope the Irish will show they are worthy of liberty by not allowing themselves to be lured by a few paltry concessions. We exhort them to continue the struggle, without truce or mercy, to reconquer their independence. We have not to trouble ourselves with the means by which this transformation will be effected ... even if some excesses are to be feared and deemed necessary, we should not indulge in hypocritical lamentations on the fate of privileged victims of this defence of property based on confiscation and fraud.

Nearly all the foreign press saw the event in political terms. The *Golos* of St Petersburg wrote: 'The movement is political and not entirely agrarian, and there is a secret party behind the Land League which aims at nothing short of overthrowing English authority'. *Die Nationale Zeitung* of Berlin commented likewise: 'There is no doubt here we have a political murder ... it is traceable to men who desire to carry on the movement till their country is sundered from Great Britain'. *Le Rappel* of Paris remarked: 'It is not so much a political and social insurrection, as a war of independence, that seems foreshadowed'.

Probably the best defence of the Invincibles was that which appeared in the *Dublin Irishman*, a paper owned by

the Parnellites and published beneath the shadow of Dublin
Castle, which declared:

> Without excusing crime of any character, or for any purpose,
> we hold that aggression is always followed by retaliation, and
> that repression is invariably the cause of outrage. It is not in
> Ireland alone that hostility on one side begets enmity on the
> other. Human nature is the same everywhere. No nation suf-
> fers injury without making an effort in its own defence. The
> English people ought to remember that we did not begin the
> bloody strife which has lasted for seven hundred years. Let
> them remember it was they who first declared war upon the
> people of this country ... Year after year for centuries, the
> English forces perpetrated many outrages in the catalogue of
> crime. As the Irish race could not submit to murder, robbery,
> and conquest, it fought and struggled against the stream of
> invasion which continued until recent days. Thus the war has
> been brought down to our own time, not of our own will but
> because the rapacity of the invaders was never satisfied.

A Matter of Timing

The assassination of Burke and Cavendish was publicly condemned by Parnell as 'murder most foul'. But the condemnation could only have been a veneer. Parnell was undoubtedly well aware that the temporary conversion of the British
Government to conciliatory tactics, demonstrated by his
own release and the release of his colleagues from Kilmainham, was only a tactical conversion, simply because the
Forster policy of extreme oppression was not meeting with
success. As he said himself in 1880, Parnell was not averse to
the use of secret physical force or to using the Constitution
for his own ends, nor would he have been squeamish about
the methods employed. He did not object to Monsieur Henri
Rochefort, whom he once visited in order to get the aid of
his powerful voice for Ireland, when the latter wrote in
l'Intransigent after the assassinations 'The cannon is the
ultima ratio of kings and the dagger is the *ultima ratio* of subjects'. Parnell in his own way stood for defiance, and there
cannot be the slightest doubt that had the assassinations
been carried out after the murder of the widowed mother,

Mary Deane, and the young girl, Ellen McDonagh, at Belmullet in October 1881, or at any time during the previous six months, while Parnell and other leaders were imprisoned without trial in Kilmainham, and resentment against British oppression was at fever pitch throughout Ireland, Joe Brady and the Invincibles would have been hailed as saviours, and have gone down in history like the legendary William Tell, as tyrannicides who risked all to liberate their country from foreign tyranny.

6

'Don't go to see Tim Healy'

1916–1921 IRA

PART 1: 1916 — Turning Point in History

It would be impossible to understand the insurrection of 1916 and the events that followed logically from it, without taking account of Ireland's history. Irish history, particularly over the previous century, made the insurrection inevitable, and the sea of change brought about by the insurrection, determined modern Ireland.

Ireland is only a small country, but with a long history of political independence, separate language and culture, going back to well before the time of Christ. Its evolution during the first millennium was orderly by comparison with other nation states in Europe, following the break up of the Roman Empire. In the twelfth century, however, Ireland became the victim of England's lust for power and expansion. A consistent effort was made by England over succeeding centuries to destroy Ireland's separate nationality and to Anglicise her people as far as possible. By the end of the seventeenth century the conquest had been largely completed in the material sense. Practically all the property of the country had been transferred into the hands of a dominant conquering minority, and the native population constituting about 80% of the total, had been reduced to a subject class. In 1800, England took the final step and forcibly annexed the country as part of the United Kingdom, making the entire Irish population into British subjects. It was this last act, together with Britain's determination to reduce Ireland to the level of a British satellite, which provided a moral justification for every revolt against British rule since then, including the current revolt in the part of Ireland still occupied by British forces.

By the start of the twentieth century the subjugation was, to all outward appearances, a near total success. Queen Victoria visited Dublin for twenty-two days (4–26 April 1900) and was greeted everywhere with speeches and addresses of welcome by reception committees, schools and hospitals – Catholic as well as Protestant. Whenever she ventured forth in her royal carriage, the crowds lined the streets in their thousands to greet her. Dublin Corporation gave her a hearty welcome at the city boundary. The Catholic Church in the person of His Eminence Cardinal Logue, Primate of all Ireland and Archbishop of Armagh, dined with her in the Viceregal Lodge.

The poor of Ireland joined the British army in their thousands and the names of the Royal Dublin Fusiliers on the inside of the memorial arch at the north-west corner of St Stephen's Green testify to the hundreds who died in the defence of the empire at Ladysmith and elsewhere during the Boer war (1899–1902).

The final piece of Land Purchase legislation was being prepared to enable farmers to become owners of their holdings, and a highly conservative class of strong farmers appeared to be getting more numerous all the time. The unionists, fully aware of their superior position, were loyal, as always, to king and empire.

Fenianism appeared to be dead to all but the faithful few, and nationalists generally seemed to have silently accepted the inevitability of conquest. Even Home Rule, which had been the cause of so much fuss in the closing decades of the last century, was now declared to be 'as dead as Queen Anne'. Truly could Mary Colum write about the turn of the century: 'The country I grew up in had all the marks of a conquered country and some of the habits and manners of an enslaved country'. The writings of her contemporaries, Percy French (1854–1920), James Joyce (1882–1941) and others, would seem to bear out her comments.

Home Rule

In the first years of this century, therefore, Ireland was a quiet and servile place. In 1906, however, the Conservative Government in England was defeated and a new reforming Liberal administration came into power. In return for support from the Irish Parliamentary Party following the second general election of 1910, the new Government promised to revive the question of Home Rule. Accordingly, in April 1912, the third Home Rule Bill was introduced, and a political chain reaction was set in motion which has not yet worked itself through to any logical conclusion. It was called home rule, but in reality it was no more than glorified local government.

At a representative meeting in Dublin on 31 March 1912, eleven days before the introduction of the new Bill, serious reservations about it were expressed by nationalists of different shades of opinion. Nevertheless, they were reluctantly prepared to give it a trial. Padraic Pearse who was present at the meeting, said that he also was prepared to give Redmond a last chance to get a genuine Home Rule measure enacted, as a stage on the way to full independence, but warned: 'If we are cheated once more there will be red war in Ireland'.

The Bill, introduced in the Commons on 11 April, proposed to give Ireland restricted control over certain day-to-day local matters, but all the substantive powers of an independent state were still denied. It proposed to establish an Irish legislature consisting of the King of England and two Houses, of which the Senate (the upper house) was to consist of forty members. The head of the Government would not be the head of the party or combination of parties, with the most seats; he would be the Lord Lieutenant, appointed by the King of England. The Lord Lieutenant would choose his own ministers, senators and judges. Matters concerning the army, navy, police, peace and war, foreign affairs, treaties, extradition, treason, external trade, navigation, merchant shipping, coinage and legal tender, customs and excise (with minor exceptions) and taxation – all such matters were to remain under the control of the Westminster Parliament. Ultimate control over matters to be delegated was also to remain with the Westminster Parliament, so that, in effect, a complete veto on all legislation of the Home Rule Parliament was given to the Lord Lieutenant.

In all vital respects, the Bill fell far short of what even the most conservative nationalists were expecting. Nevertheless, the Tories in England were quick to see how it could be used for their own party advantage. They knew that the unionists in both Ireland and England could be roused to violent opposition by playing the 'Orange Card'. Given sufficient public agitation, they hoped to precipitate a general election, get the Liberals out of office and get themselves back into power once again. For two full years, therefore, they worked unceasingly to bring this about. From December 1912 onwards, they masterminded the organisation, arming and training the Ulster Volunteers and a similar private army in England, for the sole purpose of defying the law and overthrowing the Government; they preached subversion in the Commons and in the constituencies; they conspired with senior army officers to paralyse from within the disciplined action of the British army; they schemed to get the House of Lords to refuse to pass the annual Army Bill so that theoretically there would be no British army at all in existence after 30 April 1914; they suborned the press; they secretly collaborated in the illegal importation of 35,000 rifles and 2,500,000 rounds of ammunition at Larne on 24 April 1914 in order to intimidate Parliament and force the resignation of the Liberal Government.

Partition

The 'rebellion' thus organised was an obvious treasonable
conspiracy. It did not, however, have the desired effect of
forcing the Liberals out of office – it did much worse. It
forced the Liberal Government to abandon their own Bill
which had already passed its third reading in the Commons
and now required only the final reading in the Commons,
following its return from the Lords, and the Royal Assent,
before it passed into law. In the face of the armed challenge
engineered by the Tories, and the threat of politically organised rebellion in the army, the Liberal Government surrendered. On 12 May 1914, a mere eighteen days after the landing of arms at Larne, Lloyd George, Chancellor of the Exchequer, announced to the Commons that before the Home
Rule Bill came into operation, an amending Bill, excluding
part of Ulster from its provisions, would be introduced. The
Tories had succeeded. Partition was born.

It was not the outcome Carson and his colleagues in
Ulster had worked for, over the previous two years. They
did not want a partitioned Ireland. They wanted Home Rule
for no part of Ireland. As J.B. Armour, a Presbyterian minister from Ballymoney, said at the time, 'The fear that the
management of the state machinery will not remain in the
hands of the descendants of the ascendancy party is perhaps
the strongest factor in opposition to Home Rule'. How bitterly Carson felt about being used by the Tories in their
campaign to kill Home Rule is clear from his speech in the
House of Lords on 14 December 1921, a week after the signing of the Anglo-Irish Treaty of 1921:

> I was in earnest. I was not playing politics. I believed all this.
> What a fool I was. I was only a puppet and so was Ulster, and
> so was Ireland in the political game that was to get the Con-
> servative Party into power.

Neither was a partitioned Ireland the outcome sought by
Redmond. The proposed amendment of the Home Rule Bill
marked the end of his efforts to secure, by peaceful means,

even a tiny measure of nominal freedom for all Ireland. All shades of nationalist opinion condemned his acceptance of it. His own Parliamentary colleague, William O'Brien, said:

> This Act will be born with a rope around its neck. It is not even intended to be enforced ... We regard this Bill as no longer a Home Rule Bill, but as a Bill for the murder of Home Rule such as we have understood it all our lives, and we can have no hand, act or part in the operation ... There is some-thing heart-breaking in the thought that the people ... lighted their bonfires for the passage of Home Rule without the slightest suspicion that they were all the time celebrating their own con-donation of Partition.

William Martin Murphy wrote a pamphlet condemning the Act. Arthur Griffith, Eoin MacNeill, and Pearse were loudly against it. In the words of Dorothy Macardle, 'Partition was an issue on which the All-for-Ireland League, Sinn Féin, Irish Labour, and the most uncompromising Separatists were at one. It was unthinkable. Yet the will of the Irish people was impotent to avert it – unless, possibly, by the force of arms'. Ireland had been cheated again and the movement towards another armed confrontation between militant nationalists and Britain, of which Pearse had given public warning in 1912, now moved inexorably ahead.

The Volunteers

As far as the ordinary people were concerned, all this Parliamentary debate about Home Rule was remote. There was little discussion on the subject, except among unionists. Tom Barry states in his book, *Guerrilla Days in Ireland*, that he never heard of it before he went away to join the British army in 1915. To the common people, it would make no real difference. The king's representative, the Lord Lieutenant, the British army, the RIC, and Dublin Castle would all continue to function as at present. Ireland would remain part of the British empire and Irish people would still be British subjects. True, the Irish Volunteers had been founded in November 1913 to be available, as the inaugural manifesto proclaimed, 'as a prominent element in the National life under a National Government', but 'Their duties [would] be defensive and protective, and they [would] not contemplate either aggression or domination'. Large numbers enrolled, but the great majority of them looked upon the movement as merely an adjunct to the Irish Parliamentary Party.

Soon, however, the whole question of Home Rule was to be overshadowed by a much larger event. The First World War broke out on 4 August 1914. Three weeks later, the Supreme Council of the Irish Republican Brotherhood met under the presidency of Tom Clarke at 25 Parnell Square, and decided to use the opportunity of the war 'to rise in insurrection against England'. The attendance included Clarke, Seán MacDermott, Padraic Pearse, Eamonn Ceannt, Arthur Griffith, Seán T. O'Kelly and others. Clarke had come back to Ireland from America in 1909 for the specific purpose of reactivating this secret oath-bound body and to be on the spot to organise a rebellion when the tension in Europe erupted into the open war he had correctly foreseen. On 20 September 1914, Redmond made a speech at Woodenbridge, declaring: 'It would be a disgrace for ever to Ireland if Irishmen refrained from fighting wherever the firing extends', and urged the Volunteers to join the British army, 'to fight for the defence of the highest interests of religion, of morality and right'. Eoin MacNeill accused him of selling out on the national question, and the Volunteer movement split. Some 150,000 went with Redmond and became the National Volunteers. A minority of 11,000 or 12,000 remained in the Irish Volunteers and re-organised under MacNeill.

In September also, the Supreme Council of the Irish Republican Brotherhood created the fourth Military Council with the immediate objective of securing control of the Volunteers and preparing for insurrection. Clarke, MacDermott, Joseph Plunkett and Pearse belonged to it. All except Clarke moved quickly into key positions in the re-organised Volunteers. Pearse became Director of Organisation. Plunkett specialised in military planning. MacDermott scoured the country opening new branches and enrolling new members. For tactical reasons, Clarke kept his head down and did not join the Volunteers. He was an unrepentant Fenian with a long prison record and was well known to the police. It was considered that it would be bad policy for him to join, lest his membership should attract undesirable attention from the police towards a body which was still legal and above board, and which Clarke was hoping to utilise for the purpose of the planned insurrection. He felt that this work could best be done through the IRB cabal which was now moving into positions of control in the Volunteers.

Tom Clarke – The Hidden Hand

It has been admitted by all who were familiar with the events of that time, that Clarke was the hidden hand behind the rebellion of 1916. P.S. O'Hegarty who, after Clarke's execution, edited *Glimpses of an Irish Felon's Prison Life*, says, 'More than any other man, he was responsible for the insurrection'. Seán T. O'Kelly, who was well acquainted with all the leaders of 1916 and of the parts played by each, wrote:

> If any one man could be said to be responsible for the inspiration of Easter Week, or for the carrying through successfully of the resolution to revolt – credit for that must be given to Tom Clarke. Clarke can truthfully be described as the man above all others, who made the Easter Rising. He, it was, who inspired it originally, and he, it was, who, in broad outline, laid the plans. To Seán MacDermott must be given the credit for filling in these plans – for seeing to the successful carrying out of the details necessary for such an undertaking.

Of the others, Seán T. wrote:

> James Connolly was the driving force. As well as being a man of brains and highly cultivated intelligence, he was in everything a man of action. If it were not for the insistence of Connolly, the Rising might not have taken place just exactly at that time. He, with his great yearning for freedom for his native land and for that liberty which would give a chance to Ireland to work out a worthy social system for the downtrodden, was restless and eager and insistent that the Rising

should come off at the earliest possible moment. Padraic
Pearse, probably the ablest and most inspiring figure of that
time ... symbolised in himself the unity of ideal, of the different races that go to make up the Irish Nation ... MacDonagh,
Kent and Plunkett were all of them men of high intellectual
attainments ... Joseph Plunkett, who was younger than all the
others, was a student of wide international culture. Despite his
delicate health, he took an active part in all the deliberations
and preparations for the Rising, and even undertook dangerous and arduous journeys over the continent necessary for the
working out of the plans.

By the end of 1914, preparations for the Rising had got
under way, particularly in the Dublin area. There, the Volunteers had a certain number of rifles brought in at Howth
the previous July. They were thus able to have regular drill-
ing and rifle practice. Outside Dublin, however, there was as
yet little movement. According to one who played a prominent part in the subsequent struggle for independence, the
Volunteer organiser had an uphill fight trying to convince
even nationalistic people like himself of the need, reality or
use of a Volunteer organisation. 'People talk nowadays,' he
records, 'of the conflicting orders of 1916 and the might have
beens'. Had the orders agreed been clear and explicit, there
would have been here and there throughout the country an
attempt at fighting, but little more, for there was no country-
wide organisation, very few arms and no general will to
fight.

The Nevertheless, preparations moved ahead in complete
secrecy within the inner circle of the Secret Military Council
of the IRB. Provisional dates in 1915 had been fixed for a
rising but each had to be postponed for one reason or another, so that when the Rising did in fact occur, on Easter
Monday 1916, it took the country entirely by surprise.

The initial reaction everywhere was one of shock and
disbelief. Apart from a few minor skirmishes in the prov-
inces, fighting was confined almost entirely to Dublin city.
The insurrection lasted from noon on Monday 24 April until
3.30p.m. on Friday 29 when Pearse surrendered to Brigadier-
General Lowe in Parnell Street. The Volunteers had made

their gesture. In a tribute to the men who fought under him, Pearse, as Commander-in-Chief of the Army of the Irish Republic and President of the Provisional Government, said in the manifesto issued by him on Friday morning:

> If they do not win this fight, they will at least have deserved to win it. But win it they will, although they may win it in death. Already they have won a great thing. They have redeemed Dublin many shames, and made her splendid among the names of cities ... If we accomplish no more than we have accomplished, I am satisfied. I am satisfied that we have saved Ireland's honour ... For my part, as to anything I have done in this, I am not afraid to face either the judgment of God or the judgment of posterity.

However, the people in the streets did not understand, and had little praise for the rebels. As they were led away after the surrender, bystanders in O'Connell Street spat on them. On the night of the surrender, an RIC sergeant announced the fact to an audience at a circus in Kanturk, and the news was greeted with acclamation. The reaction all over the country was much the same.

Summary execution of the leaders was carried out within days – Pearse, Clarke and Thomas MacDonagh on 3 May; Plunkett, Edward Daly, Michael O'Hanrahan and Willie Pearse on 4 May; John MacBride on 5 May; Eamonn Ceannt, Michael Mallin, Con Colbert and Seán Heuston on 8 May; Thomas Kent on 9 May; Seán MacDermott on 12 May, and on the same date, a wounded man who had to be carried to his place of execution on a stretcher and strapped to a chair to be shot – James Connolly. The king's loyal subjects could be happy that the rebellion was put down quickly and effectively. The gravel was raked smoothly over the quick-lime graves in Kilmainham. Hundreds were safely tucked away in English prisons, and General Sir John Maxwell could report that the disloyalty of the rebels was widely repudiated and abhorred. Their action was a stab in the back to Britain in time of war. Their execution was a just penalty and was designed to strike such terror in the hearts of the disloyal minority as would put all thought of rebellion out of their minds for at least another generation, and teach them once again, what had so often been emphasised to them before, that subjection to British rule was their destiny.

Execution of Prisoners of War

There were others, however, who thought differently. George Bernard Shaw wrote:

> My own view is that the men who were shot in cold blood, after their capture or surrender, were prisoners of war, and that it was therefore, entirely incorrect to slaughter them. The relation of Ireland to Dublin Castle is, in this respect, precisely that of the Balkan States to Turkey, of Belgium or the City of Lille to the Kaiser, and of the United States to Great Britain ... an Irishman resorting to arms to achieve the independence of his country is doing only what Englishmen will do, if it be their misfortune to be invaded and conquered by the Germans in the course of the present war.

'It is not murderers who are being executed,' said John Dillon MP, 'it is insurgents who fought a clean fight, a brave fight'. In the course of a letter to General Maxwell, Dr O'Dwyer, Bishop of Limerick, wrote, 'Personally I regard your action with horror, and I believe that it has outraged the conscience of the country'.

Already the policy of General Maxwell was having the opposite effect to that intended. When news of the wanton executions broke, it initially shocked the ordinary people into silence but it was an ominous silence. Then, as the killings were dragged out over several days, the further announcements roused first the people's pity, and then their rage. It was, however, a gradual not an instant or complete reversal of their initial opinion. There were then, as now, plenty who argued that the insurrection was a mistake, that Home Rule was on the way, and that Ireland would get her independence when the war was over. It took time for the ordinary people to realise that the Bill proposed in May 1914 would, as William O'Brien had declared, only murder Home Rule, deny independence and partition Ireland. It thus became the detonator that precipitated the insurrection.

It is now seventy-seven years since that gallant venture. It has had its critics, yet nobody has been able to besmirch the memory of those who took part in it. As to the criticism that the rebels had no mandate, it has to be stated that if that were accepted as a valid objection, freedom-fighters everywhere from Lexington to the Bastille could be condemned, and no oppressed people could ever gain their liberty. The view that the rebellion was engineered solely by Pearse because he believed that a blood sacrifice was needed to redeem the nation is also incorrect. It ignores the well-established fact that the insurrection was a carefully-planned military operation, organised over a long period by the secret military council of the Irish Republican Brotherhood (of which Pearse was just one member). It was inspired mainly by Clarke – with the support of MacDermott, Connolly and Pearse, but it would undoubtedly have taken place even if Pearse had not been a participant in it.

In the final analysis, despite the criticisms, 1916 will always stand as the most memorable event in the history of the Irish people's struggle for independence. At the time, Ireland was and had been for many generations, a conquered nation. But the finality of that conquest had never been recognised by all the people. Always there was a minority who regarded subjection as slavish, and challenged it repeatedly in open revolt. The rebellion of 1916 was one such challenge and without doubt the most daring and most effective in changing the course of history. It should be judged against the circumstances of the time, the overwhelming odds it had to confront, and what it actually achieved. It restored to the common people the courage to stand up for their freedom. Over the ensuing years, it broke the spell of national inanition and made clear to all that Ireland would never again be quiescent under foreign rule.

PART 2: 'The Murder Gang'?

After the rising, the Volunteers gradually became known as the Army of the Irish Republic, the IRA. Night after night, organisers went from parish to parish in town and country reviving dormant companies and setting up new ones. In a remarkably short time the organisation became as widespread and prepared as anything of its kind anywhere. Those who carried out the work did it without pay or reward and lived entirely off the generosity of a very small group of people. Side by side with the organisation of the military arm, the political party, which took the name of Sinn Féin, was also being developed. In most cases, brigade areas and political constituencies coincided.

At the outset, the IRA, outside Dublin had few arms. The weapons to be used against the British later on had, therefore, to be taken from them in the first instance. In the country districts the only rifles available were in the hands of the RIC and, from the attempts to secure these by swift and sudden action, developed the ambush and guerrilla tactics. There was no organised Quartermaster's Department from which arms or supplies could be obtained in the normal way. GHQ was essentially only a co-ordinating body, and each brigade had to rely on its own resources. It also had to develop its own strategy and tactics which were not related to any overall strategy. This looseness of organisation was a source of strength during the period of the fight with the British as, if one area was inactive or suffered a setback, it did not affect the activities or morale in other areas.

Being a guerrilla army based on local areas and supported by the local people, a vital part of the IRA organiser's work was to align the minds of the people with the mind of the IRA. He had to convince people of the soundness of policy, and of ultimate success. It had to be got across that the purpose of the war was to make British government in Ireland impossible; to ensure that the king's writ ran nowhere beyond the points of supporting British bayonets; to do this with the minimum loss of Irish lives, and to keep a fighting force in existence until the end of hostilities. A consequence of making British government impossible meant that *pari passu* with the decline of the British system, an alternative Sinn Féin police and court system had to be built on which the people could depend for justice and protection of rights.

Thus loosely organised, the IRA developed gradually throughout 1917 and 1918 along lines broadly suited to its purpose. It was not an implement for war like the ordinary military forces of a nation. It was the nation. It has been described as 'the spearpoint of the uprising of a people'. It had its roots in an age-old tradition of resistance. It was shaped and conditioned by a long-continued underground organisation, and was brought into being by the inspiration of Easter Week. By the end of 1918, there were units all over the country, but as yet there was no fighting. Were it not for the autocratic action of the British at that time, it might never have been employed at all.

Verdict of the Ballot Box

On 14 December 1918 there was a general election which gave Britain its opportunity. Sinn Féin's election manifesto advocated the establishment of an Irish Republic as proclaimed in 1916, firstly, by withdrawing the Irish representation from the British Parliament, and by denying the right and opposing the will of the British Government or any other foreign Government to legislate for Ireland; and secondly, by making use of any and every means available to render impotent the power of England to hold Ireland in subjection by military force or otherwise.

Sinn Féin swept the board at the polls gaining 73 seats (70%) out of a total of 105. The unionists won 26 seats (24.5%) and the Irish Parliamentary Party were practically wiped out, retaining only 6 seats (5.5%). If the will of the Irish people meant anything to the British, nothing could have been clearer and more decisive. This was the time for them to leave Ireland and respect the verdict of the ballot box. However, Britain had no intention of respecting the verdict of the ballot box and proceeded immediately to frustrate it. The response, as enunciated by Birkenhead, was to use such terrorism as would crush the resurgent nation, break Sinn Féin and teach the Irish people that subjection to England was their inevitable destiny. The full weight of the British army and the RIC was to be employed immediately to prevent the First Dáil – which met on 21 January 1919 – from functioning. Additional military force – guns, armoured cars, lorries and troops – was poured in to strengthen the existing garrison. On 10 September 1919, the Dáil itself was suppressed as 'a dangerous association'.

The British response left only two alternatives to the Irish people: either to renege on the decision of the electorate and meekly accept a passive rôle under further British subjugation, or to abide by the decision of the people and play an active rôle in defending the institutions authorised by the people. It was the latter alternative, forced upon the people by the British contempt for democracy, which fuelled the IRA campaign between mid-1919 and mid-1921. If the British Government was determined to make it impossible for the Dáil to function in Ireland, the IRA's reaction was to make it equally impossible for the British Government to function in Ireland, at least in so far as their resources would permit. The battle of wills continued until an impasse was finally reached and a truce was declared in June 1921.

In the pursuit of their objective, the guerrilla campaign conducted by the IRA was much more successful than the opponents of the War of Independence care to admit. It began with attacks on RIC barracks, patrols and other targets likely to result in the capture of arms. Some daring actions by small groups of volunteers, armed with no more than revolvers and a few hand grenades, were undertaken in the first year of the campaign. Seán Hogan was rescued from his military escort at Knocklong railway station in May 1919. The Viceroy, Lord French, was attacked by a party of eleven volunteers from the Tipperary and Dublin Brigades at Ashtown in December 1919, and fortuitously escaped with his heavily armed military escort under a hail of revolver bullets. By early 1920, attacks on police barracks had become more and more frequent, and police in isolated stations which could not be protected had to be withdrawn to central barracks. Over 300 of these abandoned barracks went up in flames in a single night in April 1920. At the same time, almost every income tax office in the country was raided also and put out of action or burned to the ground.

The British Government's response was swift. On 20 March 1920, Tomás MacCurtain, Lord Mayor of Cork and Officer Commanding Cork Number 1 Brigade IRA, was murdered by hooded men with blackened faces and turned-up collars, at the door of his bedroom, in the presence of his wife. The coroner's jury found that the Lord Mayor was 'wilfully murdered under circumstances of most callous brutality; that the murder was organised and carried out by the Royal Irish Constabulary, officially directed by the British Government'. Three inspectors of the RIC and some unknown members of the force were named by the jury as being responsible for the murder but nobody was brought to justice for the crime. At the end of the month, General Sir Nevil Macready was appointed Commander-in-Chief of all British forces in Ireland and given practically a free hand to suppress rebellion 'by whatever means may be requisite'. Around the same time, a new armed force was hastily organised in England and sent across to assist the RIC in the suppression of rebellion. There was a shortage of RIC uniforms for the new force, and they had to be dressed in khaki trousers and items of black police equipment, such as black hats and belts, whence their name. Shortly afterwards, still another force, named the Auxiliaries, was organised and sent to Ireland to assist in the oppression. Sir Hamar Greenwood was appointed Chief Secretary for Ireland, and Major-General Sir Hugh Tudor became chief of police.

These new arrivals from England were told through their official organ, *The Weekly Summary*, that the IRA was 'a gang of criminals under whose terrorism the people tremble[d]', that 'they belong[ed] to a race of congenital murderers outside the pale of humanity, to whom the ordinary rules of civilised warfare [could] not be applied', that 'their military operations [were] wanton atrocities', that 'the rope and the bullet [were] too good for them', and that De Valera 'belong[ed] to a race of treacherous murderers', that he had 'a fancy for ditch murders ... and if the fellow had a thousand lives they would be less than dung'. They were urged to make life 'an appropriate hell for rebels'.

'An appropriate hell for rebels'

For the next twelve months the forces of the Crown certainly did their best to carry out that last instruction until, in March 1921, General Sir Hubert Gough, Commander of the Fifth Army in the First World War, felt obliged to declare:

> Law and order have given place to a bloody and brutal anarchy in which the armed agents of the Crown violate every law in aimless and vindictive and insolent savagery. England has departed further from her own standards, and further from the standards even of any nation in the world, not excepting the Turk and Zulu, than has ever been known in history before.

Things got hotter and hotter as the year 1920 progressed, until eventually the country found itself in the middle of a wearing guerrilla war, waged along the country roads or in the streets of towns and cities, or against strongly defended police barracks. Each day brought news of fresh engagements in one part of the country or another.

In the rural areas the ambush of convoys of Tans and military became commonplace. Special units of the IRA – the Flying Columns – were organised and maintained on fulltime active service for such operations. Column commanders selected their own targets and their own time and place of attack, and thus maintained the initiative. There were many major ambushes and hundreds of minor ones. Roads were trenched or blocked at selected spots where a convoy was expected to pass and where it could be halted and successfully attacked from adjacent covered positions. Attacks were normally short, and decisive. Surprise, speed and ability to get safely away were the essentials for success. Reprisals were commonplace when military reinforcements later arrived at the scene. Houses in the vicinity were burnt down. Lorries and armoured vehicles, loaded with troops and Tans, careered recklessly through adjoining towns and country, discharging guns at passers by and at people working in the fields. Casualties were inevitable.

The conflict was widespread. On 22 September, three towns in Clare were shot up, looted and set on fire, and civilians were deliberately shot by the troops. On the same night, John Lynch of Kilmallock was murdered by military in his room in the Royal Exchange Hotel in Dublin. On 28 September, Mallow military barracks was attacked by the IRA. Twenty-seven rifles, two machine guns and a large quantity of ammunition were captured. Some hours later, the town was sacked by troops from Buttevant and Fermoy. On 14 October, in a vicious exchange of fire with a contingent of British troops and Auxiliaries in Talbot Street in Dublin, Seán Treacy and two British Intelligence officers, Lieutenant Price and Sergeant Christian, were shot dead. Two civilians were also killed and a number were severely wounded. On 25 October, Terence MacSwiney, Lord Mayor of Cork and Commandant First Cork Brigade of the IRA, died in Brixton prison after 74 days on hunger strike. Over the next month, 17 of Collins' men were taken out and shot by what Brigadier-General Crozier, Commandant of the Auxiliaries, described as General Wilson's 'first sub rosa murder gang'. On 20 November, the body of a murdered priest, Father Michael Griffin, was discovered in a Galway bog with a bullet wound in his head. On Sunday, 21 November, Collins responded and had 14 suspected British spies living in Dublin executed in their homes by members of the Dublin Brigade. In the afternoon, reprisal came. Lorries of Black and Tans surrounded Croke Park and opened fire on a crowd of 6,000 to 7,000 people who were watching a football match. The firing lasted about ten minutes, while the people tried frantically to escape. By the time it stopped, twelve people had been shot dead, sixty wounded by bullets, and hundreds trampled and injured in the stampede. Some time around midnight on 21 November, Dick McKee – Commandant of the Dublin Brigade, Peadar Clancy – Vice Commandant, and Conor Clune – a Volunteer from Clare who had been arrested some twenty-four hours previously, were shot in Dublin Castle. On 28 November, 16 Auxiliaries were killed in an ambush at Kilmichael, Co. Cork. On 11 December, Cork city was burnt and looted by Auxiliaries and Tans as a reprisal for a local ambush. Most of the shops on one side of Patrick Street and many of the public buildings in the city, including the City Hall, were burnt to the ground. On 15 December, the seventy-three-year-old parish priest of Dunmanway, Canon Magner, and Timothy Crowley were shot dead by an Auxiliary officer from Macroom.

Above is only a fraction of the terrorist measures taken by the military and police to crush Sinn Féin during the last six months of 1920, and of the counter measures taken by the IRA to defend it. Nearly every town in Ireland suffered burning, looting and sacking, many of them more than once. In a statement of autumn 1920, the Irish hierarchy wrote:

> On a scale truly appalling have to be reckoned countless indiscriminate raids and arrests in the darkness of the night, prolonged imprisonments without trial, savage sentences from tribunals that command and deserve no confidence, the burning of houses, town-halls, creameries, and crops, the destruction of industries to pave the way for want and famine – by men maddened by drink and bent on loot – the flogging and massacre of civilians, all perpetrated by the forces of the Crown, who have established a reign of frightfulness which, for murdering the innocent and destroying their property, has a parallel only in the horrors of Turkish atrocities or in the outrages of the Red Army in Bolshevik Russia.

Dozens of innocent people were shot dead in random and indiscriminate escapades. Prisoners captured in combat or taken into custody following raids were often tortured while in custody. In July 1920, two prisoners, Patrick Harte and Tom Hales, were tortured in Bandon Military Barracks, not by Black and Tans but by British army officers, until one of them – Harte – became insane and ended up in an asylum. Kevin Barry was tortured in Mountjoy prison before being hanged on 1 November 1920. Ernie O'Malley was tortured within an inch of his life, in an effort to make him answer questions, after capture in December 1920. His captors broke his toes by stamping on them. He was jabbed with bayonets, beaten in the face, half choked, and a red hot poker was held before his eyes until his eyelashes burnt. He arrived in Kilmainham prison in such a condition that his comrades did not know him. There were hundreds of similar cases.

'We have murder by the throat'

Speaking at the Guildhall Banquet in London on 9 November 1920, Lloyd George left his listeners in no doubt as to what the British Government thought about the 'Murder Gang', as he called the IRA, who were engaged in mortal combat defending the democratically arrived at decision of the Irish people of December 1918. 'We have murder by the throat', he announced with great satisfaction, and the *Weekly Summary* (official organ of the police) declared: 'If in future any member of His Majesty's forces is murdered, two members of the Sinn Féin party will be killed. And in the event of a member of the Sinn Féin party not being available, three sympathisers will be killed'. *The Times* commented, 'At the Guildhall, the Prime Minister virtually committed himself to a war upon a large section of the Irish people'.

Yet, in spite of tortures, burnings and lootings, most people remained steadfast behind the IRA. Food and shelter were provided in every parish for the flying columns. Though shooting and hanging of captured Republicans and the indiscriminate murder of civilians such as eight-year-old Annie O'Neill or Mrs Quinn, shot with a child in her arms, naturally shocked the people, the overall effect was merely to stiffen resistance against the British.

The tempo of battle accelerated ever more rapidly during the first half of 1921. Republicans, charged under the arbitrary powers conferred on the military by legislation, were executed in increasing numbers. Prominent citizens were murdered by night in selected areas, after the manner of Tomás MacCurtain in Cork the previous year. On 6 March, two men wearing goggles, with coat collars turned up and hats pulled over their eyes, forced their way into the home of Michael O'Callaghan, the former Mayor of Limerick, and shot him dead at the foot of the stairs, in the presence of his wife. The following morning it was discovered that his successor, Mayor George Clancy, had been similarly murdered in his home in the presence of his wife, at about 1.30 a.m. and that Volunteer Joseph O'Donoghue had also been murdered. On the Republican side, Crown forces were successfully attacked at Turreengarriffe, Burgatia House, Clonbanin, Crossbarry, Roscarbery and numerous other places. Two British Generals – Major-General Holmes and Brigadier-General Cummins – and many other ranks lost their lives in these attacks. As a final gesture of defiance, the Dublin Custom House, which contained among other offices those of Inland Revenue, was burnt to the ground on 25 May 1921.

Despite Lloyd George's boast the previous November that he had 'murder by the throat', and Hamar Greenwood's promise to keep the fight going until he had 'plucked the last revolver out of the last assassin's hand', the bald facts of the military situation in June 1921 seemed to point otherwise. When General Macready was given his orders in April 1920 to crush Sinn Féin and the guerrilla forces supporting it, he had under his command some 20,000 troops. By the end of 1920, total Crown forces – military and police combined – amounted to over 50,000, and by July 1921, 80,000 troops would have been in place but for the truce. Confronting this vastly superior force, there were never more than about 3,000 fighting IRA men. But such was the effect on morale of guerrilla attacks that General Macready wrote in May 1921 in a memorandum for the Government: 'Unless I am entirely mistaken, the present state of affairs in Ireland must be brought to a conclusion by October, or steps must be taken to relieve practically the whole of the troops, together with a great majority of the commanders and their staff'. General Wilson seems to have endorsed this view. At the time of the signing of the Treaty, six months later, Macready reckoned that if the war were to be renewed in December 1921, not 80,000, but 150,000 British troops would be needed to defeat the IRA. Churchill apparently maintained that by 1921, to have restored order in Ireland would have required measures on an altogether grander scale – 100,000 special troops, thousands of armoured cars, cordons of block houses, armoured patrols capable of withstanding guerrilla attacks, barbed wire to seal off cleared areas....

Lloyd George Seeks Talks with the 'Murder Gang'

Clearly, an impasse had been reached by mid-1921, and the consequences of intensifying the oppression to the level required to achieve total subjection, were politically unacceptable to Britain. Further oppression would most likely result in further condemnation by prominent people of the intensified state terror – similar to that already voiced by the hierarchy, the British Labour Commission and General Gough – without any guarantee that, apart from consideration of cost, even the most extreme oppression would ever bring the revolt to an end or that the British people would stand for it. On 24 June, Lloyd George accordingly wrote to De Valera proposing a conference with a view to peace. A truce, under which the IRA would retain their arms – a sure sign of British recognition of the latter's success – was eventually agreed, and came into effect at noon on Monday, 11 July 1921. Negotiations began shortly afterwards.

The views of prominent Republican commanders on the sudden and unexpected change in policy are worth recording. In his book, *Guerrilla Days in Ireland*, Tom Barry writes:

The British Prime Minister's invitation to the Irish leaders to attend a conference to end the war and the terms of the Truce are perhaps the best indication of all as to the success with which the Irish people waged and maintained guerrilla war. Those British Ministers who had refused so violently and viciously during the preceding years to deal with murderers, criminals and rebels had now somersaulted to approach as equals those very same leaders and to recognise the guerrilla forces as the Irish army. This startling upheaval in British policy was due, and due only, to the British recognition that they had not defeated and could not reasonably hope to defeat in the measurable future, the armed forces of the Irish nation....

Since the Treaty of Limerick in 1691 down to and including 1916 the British terms to the defeated Irish soldiers had always been unconditional surrender followed by a massacre of the Irish leaders. But now they had to deal with an army that was capable, not alone of fighting back but of actually threatening to smash their military power in Ireland in the not too distant future....

In spite of all the British efforts, the Irish Republican Army was a stronger and more effective striking force when the Truce came than at any other period in its history. In West Cork it had twice as many enrolled volunteers, three times as much armament, although the ammunition worry remained, and ten times as many toughened and experienced fighters than it had twelve months previously. Its morale and confidence had grown as that of the enemy slumped, and the Brigade had not only survived long summer days of enemy operations, but had increased its pressure and number of attacks in those later months. Never in all my contacts with senior and junior officers had I heard one doubt our ability to force eventually a British evacuation. We had no illusions about our weaknesses or the enemy's strength, and knew well the heavy price that Ireland would have to pay....

Similar views were expressed by Seán Moylan, commander of the adjoining brigade in North Cork:

The record is proof. The people stood steadfast until the British ceased to fight. The Brigade was stronger and more full of initiative on 11 July 1921 than it had been since its creation. With fresh British troops poured in; with the Auxiliaries holding the hills behind us; with search parties of thousands of men combing the countryside for the Volunteers they never lost the initiative. Rathmore, Rathcoole, Abbeyfeale and a dozen other fights that took place between March and the Truce are the proof. This was no flash-in-the-pan insurrection. It was a nation's revolt and the Volunteer organisation was the steel of its spearpoint.

The sudden offer of peace by the British came as a complete surprise to active officers such as these. Up to a few days

before the end, Lloyd George had consistently referred to
them and other IRA leaders as a gang of murderers with
whom he would never negotiate. Neither would he contemplate recognition of the Irish Republic proclaimed in 1916
and endorsed by the people in 1918. Yet, he was now in-
viting De Valera to a conference to discuss peace and to
bring with him 'any colleagues he might select'. The bar
against negotiating with Michael Collins, Director of IRA
Counter-Intelligence, Dick Mulcahy, Chief of Staff of the
IRA, and Cathal Brugha, Minister for Defence, all hitherto
regarded as too intimately associated with murder, no longer applied. In view of this somersault, the related question
naturally arose: had Lloyd George changed his mind also
about recognising his other *bête noir* – the Irish Republic? Or
could it be that intelligence coming to him from Sir Alfred
Cope, Assistant Under Secretary for Ireland, had led him to
believe that he would be able to persuade or bully Irish representatives, to give up their demands for an Irish Republic?

The IRA commanders, remote from the political ma-
noeuvring in Dublin, could get no information about these
fundamental matters. The only message from GHQ was that
the truce should be regarded as only a breathing space, that
it might end at any time, that the IRA would inevitably be
compelled to fight again and that they should hold themselves in readiness for a resumption of activities. They were
urged to believe that the negotiations in London were merely a ruse to enable the army to re-organise, strengthen and
retrain its forces. When Dick Mulcahy, Chief of Staff, visited
the North Cork Brigade in the early days of August, he
stressed the need for re-organisation and training and the
near certainty of the IRA being called upon again to fight.

'Don't go to see Tim Healy'

For some time prior to the public exchange of letters between De Valera and Lloyd George, there was an amount of
secret negotiating going on between the two sides. A number of people other than those directly involved were aware
of it. Albert Wood KC was one of them. Towards the end of

May, he visited Seán Moylan in Cork, in connection with the latter's trial, and informed him that a truce was imminent. Negotiations were going on, he said, and in six weeks time all the fighting would be over. Events were to show that he was well informed. Five weeks after the start of the truce they met again, this time in Dublin. Moylan had been elected to the Second Dáil in May, and had come to Dublin for a meeting on 16 August. He was having dinner that night in the Gresham Hotel with a business friend, when they were joined at table, first by John McLoughlin of Donegal, afterwards a senator, and later by Albert Wood. In the course of their discussions, the name of Tim Healy came up and McLoughlin, who was a friend of Healy, suggested that he (Moylan) should come with him to Chapelizod to see Tim Healy. Moylan was had worked with McLoughlin in Innishowen during the 1918 election, and consented to go along with him. As they left, Wood warned him, 'Don't go to see Tim Healy! You have certain ideals, for which you fought, and Healy is the centre of an intrigue which, if successful, will dash the hopes held by you and your comrades'. From past experience Moylan trusted Wood's judgment and reliability, and he did not go to see Tim Healy.

The fact that there was much intrigue afoot during the months immediately prior to the signing of the Treaty, and that the army was being kept in the dark about it, generated deep suspicion all around and caused a serious split in the Republican movement. The fighting men felt that they, who had borne the heat of the day, were being betrayed, and that the Republic was being abandoned by the politicians. As Liam Mellows later pointed out: 'Were it not for the Volunteer Movement, they could not talk of Ireland abroad, and if it were not for the Volunteers they could give up any idea of a Republic'. Instead of being deceived and led up the garden path with talk about the army continuing to be the Army of the Republic, had the army been trusted and told the plain truth, in the view of many men of integrity and ability who opposed the settlement of December 1921, the civil war to which it gave rise in 1922/1923 might have been avoided.

7

'Those to whom evil is done'

PART 1: Never ... ever ... even if'

The Balance of Power

For centuries, Britain had been keenly aware of the danger that any other country's domination of the European continent would present to her own ambitions to build herself, first into a strong nation state, and later on into an empire with worldwide commercial interests. Consistently, therefore, she sought to minimise this danger by maintaining a balance between rival European powers. Through skilful diplomacy, she enjoyed a large measure of success. Because of the accident of location, Ireland became a victim of this policy. Britain could not afford to let her fall at any time under the influence of any other European power who might be regarded as a threat. Whenever this was likely to happen, as with Spain during Elizabeth I's reign or with the French in later centuries, Britain took action to oppose it. Whatever the cost, Ireland had to be held either subject to, or under the influence of Britain.

However, the policy was based on the fallacy that a majority of the Irish people can be permanently forced through military oppression to accept foreign rule. From the beginning, force was the instrument of English policy. In the words of the famous attorney general, Sir John Davies, the object was: 'to root out the Irish from the soil, to confiscate the property of the septs and plant the country systematically with English tenants'. 'Confiscation' and 'Plantation' were indeed successfully applied but they produced a deep and lasting division in the nation between a minority dominant class of 'haves' (mostly Protestant) and a majority subject class of 'have nots' (mostly Catholics) who never recognised the finality of the conquest, and who, time and again, emphasised their opposition in revolt. Whenever native leaders attempted to reverse the position with help from continental powers, Britain took all possible steps to oppose them. In the sixteenth century, Spain was the opponent. The final answer to Spain's involvement was her engagement and defeat in conjunction with Irish forces at Kinsale in 1603, the forced flight of O'Neill and O'Donnell from Tyrone and Donegal, and the subsequent plantation of the province of Ulster with English and Scottish settlers. It was followed later in the century by the major confiscation and plantation of 11 million acres out of a total of some 20 million in all Ireland, under the Cromwellian Settlement. This wholesale transfer of property throughout the entire country provided the economic base for an English garrison, which constituted the foundation of English power in Ireland up to modern times. The message was clear. Neither Spain nor any other Continental power would ever be allowed to gain a foothold in Ireland if Britain could help it.

For the next two and a half centuries, France was England's principal Continental rival. It was only when Germany became a strong power and a potential threat to England's imperial interests in the late nineteenth century that the position changed and France became England's ally. Three times, their former rivalry had touched Ireland. During the Williamite wars of 1690/91, Louis XIV was the ally of James II in the latter's endeavour to recover his crown from William III. In 1782, the attempt by the garrison to establish legislative independence, at a time when France had openly allied herself with the revolting American colonies,

was regarded by England as a serious threat to her own security. In 1796 and 1798, France actually dispatched three
separate expeditions to Ireland to help the United Irishmen
in their efforts to establish an Irish Republic.

The Union – An Act of International Banditry

England's position in the face of rising French power thus
became a matter of great concern at the end of the eighteenth
century. In Pitt's view, the answer to the problem lay in the
enforced annexation of Ireland by England, and the compulsory unification of the two countries into a single kingdom.
It has been euphemistically called the union of 1800. It was
not a union at all, but rather an act of international banditry
against the wishes of the overwhelming majority of the Irish
people. England merely seized control after the defeat of the
United Irishmen in 1798, and the people had no way of pre-
venting it. Lord Byron wrote of such a union:

> Between a small nation and a great,
> between a conquered people and its conqueror,
> there can be but a sham union
> – the union of a boa constrictor with its prey.

There was no United Nations to which a nation abused by a
big power could appeal.

Pitt had his own reasons for the union and sufficient
military force to back them up. Irish nationalism, whether of
the mild type represented by the garrison 'patriots' or the
republican brand, championed by the Presbyterians of Ulster and the United Irishmen, had to be reined in, and that
could be done only by a union of the two islands. It was only
through the union that England could disabuse the garrison
of their ideas about legislative independence, and keep it allied to her side. Only through the union also, could they be
kept contented in their dominant position as landed gentry.
Industrial and commercial development of the kind spon-
sored by Grattan's Parliament had to be discouraged. It
would lead only to competition with English manufacturers,

to a growing urban population, a rising middle class and demands for more democracy with troublesome French ideas about Liberty, Equality and Fraternity. But above all, it was only through the union that militant republicanism could be kept at bay.

England would Rather Drown the Demand for Repeal in Blood

In all her negotiations with Irish leaders, Britain made it clear that she never could relax her hold on Ireland one whit because it would jeopardise her own security. Peel told O'Connell that 'all the resources of the empire would be exerted to preserve the union ... and that deprecating civil war as he did, he should hold civil war preferable to the dismemberment of the empire'. Queen Victoria affirmed from the throne that she was firmly determined under the blessing of divine providence to maintain the union. *The Times* wrote 'But even were it [The union] gall to Ireland, England must guard her own life's blood, and sternly tell the disaffected Irish "you shall have me for a sister or a subjugatrix; that is my ultimatum"'. The majority of the Irish nation sought repeal of the union by peaceful agitation under O'Connell, but England declared that, even if all Ireland demanded that measure, England would rather drown the demand in blood. The message from Palmerston, Disraeli, Salisbury and every other British Prime Minister of the century was the same.

In the various Home Rule Bills introduced for Ireland in the late nineteenth and early twentieth centuries, care was taken to ensure that Britain's interest was always fully safeguarded. The king of England was in all measures to remain the ultimate power. The king's representative or lord lieutenant was to be the head of government. The only armed forces to be permitted were the British army, navy and police. Even the Anglo-Irish Treaty of 1921 and the Government of Ireland Act 1920 left Britain's interests entirely secure. Under the former, British military forces remained on in key installations in the south – 'The Treaty Ports' – and under the latter, the British army remained established behind a new frontier in the north – the frontier of Northern Ireland; representatives of the newly established Parliament of the Irish Free State bound themselves by an oath of allegiance to the king. The British were delighted. 'We gave almost nothing,' declared Cabinet Secretary Tom Jones, joyfully over his champagne the night the Treaty was signed. The promise made to Michael Collins and the other members of the Irish delegation in regard to the future determination of the border 'in accordance with the wishes of the inhabitants' of the area was subsequently reneged upon. When the time came to honour it in 1925, Collins and Griffith were dead.

Britain's Necessity – A Moral Code!

The neutral policy adopted by Ireland during the Second World War caused some concern to Britain, particularly because of the non-availability of naval facilities in the 'Treaty Ports'. She used her influence with America in the early days of the war to block the purchase by Ireland of even modest amounts of standard military equipment. She seemed to be afraid lest Ireland would become too well armed. In his victory speech at the end of the war, Churchill made it clear what he thought about the interests of Ireland as against the interests of England. In certain circumstances, he said, he would have violated Ireland's neutrality and would have justified his action by Britain's necessity, drawing forth the memorable reply from De Valera that if this contention were to be admitted it would mean that 'Britain's necessity would become a moral code, and that when this necessity became sufficiently great, other people's rights were not to count'. 'In those circumstances,' continued De Valera, 'a like justification can be framed for similar acts of aggression elsewhere, and no small nation adjoining a great power could ever hope to be permitted to go its own way in peace'. Churchill made no answer, but his remarks clearly indicated that where Britain's interests were concerned, might would always transcend right.

Never ... ever ... even if

While the burden of the union might have to be marginally
adjusted from time to time to suit the backs of the subjects
yoked under it, it still remained a corner stone of British defence policy, and up to the Second World War, Britain apparently considered that no change could be made which
would jeopardise her security. Under the different arrangements made in 1920, 1921 and 1938, she always retained control over sufficient territory in one part or another of Ireland
to enable her to meet an attack by any power using Ireland
as a base. After the war, when NATO was being formed, the
retention of the six counties was still regarded as vital. The
confidential minutes of the British Labour Cabinet of 1949,
Number 49(4) accurately express Britain's permanent interest:

> So far as can be foreseen, it will never be to Great Britain's ad-
> vantage that Northern Ireland should form part of a territory
> outside His Majesty's jurisdiction. Indeed, it seems unlikely
> that Great Britain would ever be able to agree to this, even if
> the people of Northern Ireland desired it.

It is becoming daily more obvious that the statelet created on
11 November 1920 without the vote of a single Irish representative, unionist or nationalist, was founded on such an
undemocratic basis that it is ungovernable save with the
continued support of the British army. In partitioning the
country, Britain ignored the nationalist majorities in constituencies in Tyrone, Fermanagh, South Down, South Armagh and Derry city which had voted for self government in
every election since the secret ballot was introduced in 1872,
and insisted in keeping tens of thousands under the Union
Jack against their wishes. The dragon's teeth sewn on that
occasion have now sprung up as armed men. The seeds
planted by Bonar Law and Birkenhead and the other senior
Tories who conspired between 1912 and 1914 to subvert Parliament, to undermine the army, to finance and collaborate
in the illegal importation of arms at Larne and to engineer
the partition of Ireland for purely party political ends, are

today bearing bitter fruit. As acknowledged by Carson himself in 1921, when it was too late: 'Ireland and Ulster were only puppets in the Tory party political game that was to get the Liberals out of office and themselves into power'.

Reforming the Unreformable

The statelet engineered in 1920 was such that for fifty years the people could not change it by normal democratic means. When it finally erupted in fire and flame in the late 1960s under the weight of its own corruption, Britain belatedly decided to try to reform it, rather than to end it, in the mistaken belief that the strategic needs of the past were still relevant and that she still required control over that territory. The constitutional status of the statelet was, therefore, to be left unchanged. The Prime Minister, Captain Terence O'Neill, was urged to reform some of the worst abuses, but reform proved to be impossible. In April 1969, he resigned and was replaced by Major James Chichester-Clark. In August 1969, unionist mobs showed what they thought about reform. Armed civilians attacked nationalist ghetto areas which housed many of those agitating for an end to gerrymandering, property restraints on voting, discrimination on religious grounds in regard to employment, housing and other basic rights, while Her Majesty's Royal Ulster Constabulary and 'B' Specials stood by and did not protect the nationalists. At least seven people were killed in their homes and over one hundred dwellings in nationalist districts were burnt down in two nights.

Maintaining the Status Quo

The British Government then sent in the troops, allegedly to keep peace. Lord Cameron, who chaired the Cameron Commission, which had been appointed by the Government in January 1969 to investigate clashes between loyalists and civil rights marchers, reported wholesale bigotry and discrimination. Lord Scarman blamed the riots on the forces of alleged 'law' and 'order'. The Hunt Commission, appointed by the Government in August 1969, under the chairmanship of Lord John Hunt, discovered that the RUC was composed almost entirely of Protestants with a strong anti-Catholic bias who bracketed Catholics generally with Fenians and republicans, and regarded nearly all Catholics as disloyal to the state. The report of the commission recommended that the RUC should be relieved of all duties of a military nature and that the 'B' Specials should be disbanded. This was implemented on 1 April 1970. However, a new force, the Ulster Defence Regiment, was granted many of the old powers of the 'B' Specials, and many former 'B' Specials joined the UDR.

The British Army Move to the Offensive

In July 1970, before a single shot was fired on the nationalist side, the British army moved to the offensive. Curfew was imposed on the republican Falls Road area but not on the unionist Shankill. In March 1971, Chichester-Clark was forced to resign and the hardline anti-reformer, Brian Faulkner took over. On 9 August 1971, 365 nationalists were rounded up in the early hours of the morning, and interned without trial, in a move to put 'the men of violence' out of circulation. Before the end of the year, almost 1,000 men and women were being held without trial. All parades, marches and processions were banned. On Sunday, 30 January 1972, the Civil Rights Association proposed to hold an anti-internment march in Derry city despite the ban. The first battalion of the Parachute Regiment was sent into the city to stop the march. Within twenty minutes on that fateful Sunday evening, 13 unarmed civilians (seven of them of school-going age) were shot dead, and the same number were wounded. Ever since, it can be said that the British army is on a war footing in the six counties and its selective repression of the nationalist people has been a primary reason for the revival, and continued existence of the IRA there.

The 'reform' of the paramilitary police forces which had been so effectively used for over half a century to keep the nationalist people in subjection simply involved a rearrangement of existing personnel. The new Ulster Defence Regiment, comprising 3,000 full-time and 3,500 part-time members, was fully equipped by the British and was substantially better armed than the Specials it replaced. The RUC retained its name but its strength was more than trebled from 3,000 odd to about 10,000. It still continued to be an almost entirely Protestant force. The 'reforms' meant that the same 13,000 or so Protestants who made up the paramilitary security forces prior to the re-organisation were arranged differently and given different names. Taken in conjunction with the prison service and all others involved in security, it is estimated that roughly 30,000 people – mostly Protestant – are now engaged in policing the nationalist minority. The figure amounts to about one in fifty of the total population, or one in thirty of the Protestant section, and is growing all the time. It would be the equivalent of between a million and a million and a half for the United Kingdom as a whole.

Discrimination in Employment on Grounds of Religion

Even after twenty years of supposed reforms in employment practices, discrimination against Catholics/nationalists in the six counties continues. The second class citizens who make up a substantial proportion of the Roman Catholic population are still roughly two and a half times more likely to be unemployed or without job opportunities equivalent to their Protestant/unionist counterparts. Discrimination against them has been developed over a long period under the general direction of the Orange and Masonic Orders. It has been practised at central and local level and by the business community for generations. It is still rife in the civil service, public institutions, semi-state bodies, universities, trades unions, manufacturing, industrial and commercial sectors.

The public sector alone accounts for the employment of more than 200,000 people and is largely controlled by the civil service under the appropriate British ministers. Figures published in Belfast in 1991 by the Equality Working Group indicate the present position in some of the more important areas. In the top level of remuneration in the civil service,

85.5% of the senior posts are still held by Protestants and others[†] as against only 14.5% by Catholics. In the local service up to 90% in most areas, and in one case 100%, of senior officers and staff are stated to be Protestant and others. In the Northern Ireland Electricity Service which is a monopoly supplier, 96% of the management, senior and middle grades are Protestant and others, and in the engineering grades the figure is 97%. In the Ambulance Service 95.5% of officers and 85.9% of leading ambulance staff are Protestant and others. Even basic-grade ambulance staff do not equate to population distribution in any one of the Health and Social Services Board areas. In the fire service, 92.9% of officers, 93.3% of sub-officers and 89.7% of fire control staff are Protestant and others. In the universities, the pattern is the same. Out of a total of 2,991 employed by Queen's, 84% are Protestant and others and 16% are Catholic. In Ulster University the corresponding figures are 83.6% and 16.4% respectively, out of a total of 2,402.

All of the foregoing examples relate to areas directly funded by the British Government. Many private companies in which substantial public funds have been invested are no less discriminatory.

Such levels of discrimination in private industry would not of course be possible without the acquiescence of sections of the trade union movement. Active collaboration between some trade union organisers and management in engineering and manufacturing has made this sector of the economy notorious for its anti-Catholic working and employment practices. They include the restriction of entry of Catholic apprentices into skilled craft trades, the illegal and discriminatory use of unemployed members' lists as refer-

---

[†] In many of the reports, the religious denominations of employees are classified as unidentifiable, or as having originated outside Northern Ireland, and consequently being classifiable as non-denominational. In order that no misunderstanding of the implications of such classifications shall arise, all such classifications have been categorised in the following pages as 'Protestant and Other'; while Catholics of Northern Ireland origin have been shown in a single category.

ence points for employment, the maintenance of selective agreements designed to frustrate retention of Catholics in, or to deny their entry into, permanent employment.

Clearly, discrimination on religious grounds is as deeply entrenched in the six counties today as ever. While the British self-declared 'Never ... ever ... even if' policy remains, the selective population control achieved by such discrimination may not be altogether unwelcome to them. Without it, a growing Catholic population might eventually outnumber the unionists, and that might in turn, give rise to more trouble from nationalists. The practices which ensure that Catholic/nationalist unemployment will be kept consistently at more than twice that of Protestants/unionists, that the overwhelming proportion of the better-paid jobs will remain in the hands of Protestants and others rather than with Catholics, and that young Catholics will have to emigrate twice as fast from the six counties as their Protestant counterparts, may therefore be regarded by Britain as in her best long-term interest. It is a subtle update of Sir John Davies' policy of 'rooting out the Irish'.

The Churches and the British

The British Government, however, is never satisfied to rely on the Orange and Masonic Orders and the unionist section of six county society alone to further its interests. By direct and indirect manipulation, and naked propaganda – as in 1795–1800, 1867–90 and 1916–21 – it succeeded in persuading the Roman Catholic hierarchy to throw their weight behind the policy of repression and discrimination. Despite the fact that there was no prospect whatever of getting the corrupt Stormont system reformed by peaceful persuasion prior to its suspension (any more than the corrupt system established under the old Irish Parliament could be peacefully reformed in 1791), the Roman Catholic bishops of the north asserted in 1970 that:

Significant changes [as distinct from minor concessions aimed at defusing protest] have taken place with regard to the position of the minority in Northern Ireland during the past 18 months ... As these changes – and other vitally important changes which have been promised – take effect, there will be a genuine prospect of justice and peace and further progress by orderly means.

The repression and discrimination which still continue in the six counties today, even after twenty years of direct British rule, is an indication of how far the 'vitally important changes' that were promised, have progressed.

Apparently, the hierarchy have taken the view now, that while some Catholics may obtain employment in the state, the Catholic community as a whole cannot expect ever to obtain equal economic status with the non-Catholic community, even on a basis proportionate to their numbers. They suggest that since the boundary of the six county statelet was so drawn that the non-Catholic members would be in a permanent majority, the local Catholic community and the international community should slavishly submit to that injustice, give up looking for equality between Catholics and non-Catholics in the matter of employment, and press instead just for increased investment and more jobs generally. It is an appalling attitude, almost a modern-day echo of the teaching of bishops at the time of the Famine that starving tenants should pay their rents to the landlords, even if doing so meant allowing themselves and their children to die of hunger.

Like the politicians of today who apparently have forgotten about the unanimous declaration adopted by Dáil Éireann on 10 May 1949 (Appendix), the hierarchy seem to be more concerned with condemning those who are actively engaged in the struggle against the British in the six counties than with condemning the immoral British claim to Irish territory under the Act of Union, which is the root cause of the conflict. Nor is the immorality of the partition of the country and the trapping of tens of thousands under the Union Jack in defiance of the 1918 election result ever mentioned. Nor is the 'shoot to kill' policy, or the repeated killing of unarmed civilians by British soldiers, or the regular abuse of the nationalist population over the past twenty years, sufficiently aired at national and international level.

It is something of a recompense, however, that an Englishman and a Protestant should be able to see to the bottom of all the current propaganda and be prepared to say what the Irish hierarchy and Irish politicians should be saying. Writing at the time of the Long Kesh hunger strike in 1980, the Most Reverend Dr John Austin Baker, Anglican Bishop of Salisbury, leading Church of England theologian and Chaplain to the House of Commons summarised the position:

> No British Government ought ever to forget that this perilous moment, like many before it, is the outworking of a history for which our country is primarily responsible. England seized Ireland for its own military benefit. It planted Protestant settlers there to make it strategically secure. It humiliated and penalised the native Irish and their Catholic religion; and then, when it could no longer hold on to the whole island it kept back part to be a home for the settlers' descendants, a nonviable solution from which Protestants have suffered as much as anyone.
>
> Our injustice created the situation; and by constantly repeating that we will maintain in it so long as the majority wish it, we actively inhibit Protestant and Catholic from working out a new future together. This is the root of the violence, and the reason why the protesters think of themselves as political offenders.

Today, after almost twenty-three years of being at the receiving end of death by SAS and Paratroopers, Diplock Courts, imprisonment without trial, 'own goals' mistakes, infiltration by spies, and discovery of weapons, the Provisional IRA are stronger than ever. Such is the counterproductive effect of military oppression. The IRA are well aware that their forces cannot beat the combined military forces of the British, but they are equally well aware that the British cannot beat them. It is a stalemate situation. The thousands of voters who reject the British claim to the six counties see the British army as an army of occupation in the context of Bloody Sunday, Aughnacloy, Cullyhanna and hundreds of other assaults, and as one of the prime causes of

violence in the area. They are certain that there can be no
peace until the army is withdrawn totally from Ireland, and
Britain's 'Never ... ever ... even if' policy is abandoned.

PART 2: War of Attrition or Peace?

You Mustn't Talk with Terrorists

For years, many intelligent Englishmen – historians, writers, and publicists of all sorts – have argued that there can be no peace in the six counties until the Union Jack is hauled down and the British army is brought back to England. Successive British Governments have consistently refused even to discuss this course of action and simply give the bland reply 'You mustn't talk with terrorists'. This official policy worked well as a way of handling revolts against imperial rule all over the world, including Ireland, in the nineteenth century. As Jimmy Lowther, Chief Secretary for Ireland in the 1870s, often demonstrated, the correct way to handle a difficult problem of subjugation was to bury one's head in the sand and ignore its existence. If it did not wither away of its own accord, then send in the troops to settle it by other means. However, that was over a century ago. The evidence from everywhere now, is that this attitude will not work any more. Rebels will no longer lie down meekly, and only the removal of the cause of revolt will bring permanent peace to an area in rebellion against foreign rule.

Terms such as 'terrorists', 'murderers' and 'assassins' are now used daily by politicians and commentators on both sides of the Irish Sea in referring to those who have taken up arms against British rule in the six counties. The aim is to undermine, as far as possible, all support for rebels, and distract public attention from the aims which they embrace and the causes of rebellion. Anybody who ever took up arms in the past against the British presence in Ireland was described in similar terms. Robert Emmet and his followers were branded in 1803 as 'a bloodthirsty crew'. The 1916 rebels were called 'murderers' and 'traitors' who deserved to be executed in cold blood after their surrender. The IRA of 1920/21 were described as 'murderers', 'a murder gang', 'a gang of criminals under whose terrorism the people tremble' and 'criminals outside the pale of humanity, unworthy of being treated as human'. Sinn Féin was described as 'crime incarnate' for whose propagators 'the rope and the bullet are all too good'. Up to a few weeks before the truce in July 1921, Lloyd George was boasting that he had murder by the throat and that he would never talk with terrorists until the last revolver was plucked from the last assassin's hand. But before very long he did talk to the terrorists and, as a result of his talking, the Union Jack was hauled down and removed from southern Ireland, and peace of a sort descended – albeit 'dropping slowly'. In fact, in order to bring peace to any area in revolt against foreign rule – be it Lexington or the Baltic States, Algiers or Vietnam – there is no alternative but to talk to the 'terrorists' in that area.

British Propaganda and the Catholic Church

On 26 November 1974, Bishop Cahal Daly of Down and Connor (now Cardinal Daly) explained:

> There is no historical continuity, whatever, between the present, largely faceless, leaders of the self-styled republican movement and their honourable forebears; there is no moral continuity between their methods and those of an earlier struggle for independence.

His Lordship made no reference, however, to the atrocious crimes alleged by the hierarchy of the 1920–23 period to have been committed by these 'honourable forebears', which caused the Church authorities at that time to excommunicate them from their church. Nevertheless, the historical misrepresentation in the statement did not detract from its propaganda value to the British, and the British Foreign and Commonwealth Office had it printed and issued for distribution in America.

Bobby Sands, Mairead Farrell and Colleagues

Contrary to the above statement, there appears to be considerable similarity between many of today's activists and their 'honourable forbears' of an earlier struggle for independence. Bobby Sands, for example, may be compared with Terence MacSwiney in several respects. He had the same moral courage to give up life itself on hunger strike rather than allow the British Government to break his spirit and destroy his political convictions. Of himself and his colleagues, Sands wrote:

> We wish to be treated 'not as ordinary prisoners' for we are not criminals. We admit no crime unless, that is, the love of one's people and country is a crime ... We resist the attempt to criminalise us ... I am a political prisoner because I am a casualty of a perennial war that is being fought between the oppressed Irish people and an alien, oppressive, unwanted régime that refuses to withdraw from our land.

Anyone who wants to understand the character of this remarkable man and his ideas and the efforts made in Her Majesty's H Block prisons to dehumanise prisoners and break their resolve should read the published anthology of his writings. He was only twenty-seven years old when he died, and nine of those years were spent in prison.

Mairead Farrell is another remarkable volunteer. Killed with two companions in Gibraltar in 1988 by regular British soldiers in civilian attire on instructions from their leaders, she was a student at Queen's University at the time. The priest who said her funeral Mass – Fr Raymond Murray – was chaplain to Armagh prison while she was a prisoner there and knew her well. He described her as:

> cailín, gáiriúil, díograiseach, cróga
> cliste, croíúil, aigeantach, beoga.[†]

In Armagh prison she joined the first hunger strike and acted as leader of the other women prisoners. In his homily, Fr Murray said, 'For ten years in Armagh Jail, Mairead was a great and loyal friend. She was a generous companion to all the girls. They suffered a lot. Mairead herself served three extra years of punishment. It is impossible for me to prise open that world. The depth of solidarity of people who suffer together is too great to explain'. There are hundreds like her and like Bobby Sands.

[†] a laughing, devoted, brave, clever, cheerful, spirited and lively girl.

The Psychology of Resistance

Fr Murray grasped the point exactly. The depth of solidarity of people who suffer together is enormous. It is a psychological bond and those who cannot bring psychology to bear on a struggle against foreign rule will never understand the driving force behind the current resistance in the six counties. The 1916–21 struggle was also psychological. Prior to 1916, the whole of Ireland had, in the words of Mary Colum, 'all the marks of a conquered country and some of the habits and manners of an enslaved country'. The nationalist people as a whole, were treated as second class citizens – the subject class. Nearly everything worthwhile was in the hands of the unionists. But the common people had eventually had enough. The wanton execution of the 1916 leaders, the rejection of the results of the general election of 1918 and the suffering under the ensuing military oppression produced a violent reaction and deep solidarity among the ordinary people which sustained the armed rebellion of 1920/21. It was this same kind of solidarity which Fr Murray found among the prisoners in Armagh and which exists today among the tens of thousands of Sinn Féin supporters in the six counties. It expresses itself in a refusal to acquiesce ever again to British rule in Ireland.

It is not a matter of economics but rather a question of human dignity, of self esteem and of respect for one's own manhood. The poet, Eoghan Ruadh O'Sullivan, put it well, around 1780:

> Ní hé an bochtanas is measa liom
> ná bheith síos go deo
> ach an tarcaisne a leanann é
> ná leigheasadh na leoin.[†]

It would seem from many of the debates in the British Houses of Parliament that the same sort of racial contempt is still very much alive in British ruling circles today. It is

---

[†] It is not poverty nor our lowly condition that bears so hardly on us but that contempt in which we are held that is beyond our power of endurance.

vividly conveyed in the remarks attributed to Mrs Thatcher about the 'shiftless, snivelling, spineless' Irish, and about those people in the six counties who shelter and support in safe houses the 'terrorists' who murder the British security forces.

The Resistance Fighter

To understand what causes young men and women to set their feet on a dangerous road, the end of which many may never see, one must take account of what is called patriotism or love of one's people and one's country. Its meaning is not to be found in the cynic's sneer, 'the last refuge of a scoundrel' or 'True patriots we; for be it understood,/ We left our country for our country's good', but rather in the lines, 'the savage loves his native shore' or 'Breathes there the man, with soul so dead,/ Who never to himself hath said,/ This is my own, my native land!' All people feel for their own country, and no people more so than the British themselves as can be seen plainly at Armistice commemoration parades every 11 November. Yeats gives expression to the feeling in:

> I hear lake water lapping with low sounds by the shore;
> While I stand on the roadway, or on the pavements gray,
> I hear it in the deep heart's core.

and Rupert Brooke:

> .... there's some corner of a foreign field
> That is for ever England ...
> Her sights and sounds; dreams happy as her day;

The guerrilla fighter in the six counties today, with a gun in his hand, feels the same pangs for the lake waters he knew, or the flags of West Belfast or the Cleggan. But what motivates him into action is very much more substantial and immediate than just love of territory or better social conditions or revenge for the oppressions of the past. He is determined that he and his people will oppose to the limit of their capabilities, the oppression of the present, the rooting up of families and homes, the indiscriminate shooting of individuals, the killing of selected people by the sub rosa murder gangs in the SAS – successors to General Sir Henry Wilson's sub rosa murder gangs of 1920 – and the wholesale terrorisation of nationalist people in the name of 'law' and 'order'.

Today's guerrilla was born into the present situation. As a child he learned all about the killing of thirteen unarmed people in Derry city in 1972. He has very likely seen unarmed people attacked and killed in his own area with plastic bullets or live ammunition, by helmeted British soldiers in full battle order. He has witnessed the sorrow in his own or a neighbour's home at the loss of a father or a brother or some other relative. He has been through it all over a long period. Too much blood has now flowed under the bridge for him to give up the struggle. He and his comrades would rather be annihilated than surrender. If he is killed, he knows that there will be others to take his place. The young child of three years, looking into his father's open grave a while back, will grow up in due course to understand what it is all about and take up the torch. It is a war without end. It is what William Pitt, Earl of Chatham, meant when he said in the House of Lords in 1777: 'If I were an American as I am an Englishman, while a foreign troop was landed in my country, I never would lay down my arms – never, never, never', or Churchill's declaration in 1940: 'We shall defend our island, whatever the cost may be. We shall fight on the beaches. We shall fight on the landing grounds. We shall fight in the fields and in the streets. We shall fight on the hills. We shall never surrender'.

British Fight and Ireland's Right

The British fully understood and supported Churchill's declaration. If the Germans had won the last war and held back six counties in the south of England as a bridgehead for the German army and a homeland for a million Germans, the British people as a whole, would as surely have supported any armed effort made by their compatriots in the occupied counties to eject the Germans and recover control of their territory. They know that they have no more moral claim to the six counties than the Germans would have to six counties in the south of England in the hypothetical situation posed, nor than Saddam Hussein had to Kuwait following armed aggression in 1990, but as long as they have sufficient armed might to enforce their claim, the immorality of their position and the rights of the Irish people as a whole are ignored.

All British Governments are aware that Great Britain is the only power with a de facto and exercisable claim to the six counties. This derives from Article 1 of the union which provided that all the territory of Ireland became part of the United Kingdom of Great Britain and Ireland as from 1 January 1801 and for ever after. The claim is confirmed by Section 75 of the Government of Ireland Act 1920 which states that the 'supreme authority of the Parliament of the United Kingdom shall remain unaffected and undiminished over all persons, matters and things in Northern Ireland'. This fundamental claim has never been abandoned by Britain nor is it materially affected in any way by the statement of fact and right in Articles 2 and 3 of the Irish Constitution. The people in the six counties themselves have no claim at all to the territory in which they live, save as a small minority section of the total population of the United Kingdom. The Act of Union and the Government of Ireland Act 1920 are both acts of aggression against the wishes of the majority of the Irish people. They are the only two acts which enshrine a de facto claim to the six counties. The claim is backed by military force – the British army – as was the claim over the whole island of Ireland between 1800 and 1921. When the British gave up that claim in respect of twenty-six counties in 1921, peace came to that part of Ireland. The continued maintenance of the claim over the remaining six counties is the root cause of the continuing conflict today in those counties.

Nevertheless, the lie has been propagated around the world that the conflict in the six counties is a conflict between two communities of different religions, rather than a revolt against the British. The reality is, that the revolt has nothing to do with religion per se, nor is it a war between two communities. The Catholic Church as an institution was always as much anti-republican as the British Government itself. In fact, republicanism as a form of government was first preached in Ireland among the Presbyterians in Ulster. It was they who formed the first Liberty Club in Belfast in 1790, sent for Wolfe Tone the following year, founded the United Irishmen, preached that we were a nation of slaves, argued that we should rid ourselves of the British as the colonists had done in America and rise out in armed rebellion in 1798. Most of the leaders against British rule in Ireland – Tone and Lord Edward Fitzgerald, Emmet and Russell, Henry Joy McCracken of Antrim and Henry Monroe of Down, John Mitchel and Thomas Davis and many others were all Protestants, although, as Lecky says about the leaders of the United Irishmen, a large proportion of them were indifferent to theological doctrines. Their common political objective was the removal of British rule from Ireland. Emmet spoke for all that generation of rebels at his trial in 1803:

> My object and that of the provisional Government was to effect a total separation between Great Britain and Ireland; to make Ireland totally independent of Great Britain but not to let her become a dependent of France.

Believing their own Propaganda

The great difficulty with British politicians today is that many have come to believe their own propaganda about the nature of the revolt in the six counties. As a consequence, they actually believe that Tyrone, Fermanagh, South Down, South Armagh and Derry city are the same as Finchley and Yorkshire and the rest of the United Kingdom, and that young fellows in these counties and other nationalist areas, within this most disunited kingdom, who have been roughed up, shot up, beaten up, humiliated and almost shamed into the IRA are actually 'murderers' on a par with common criminals. They have deluded themselves into believing that the killing of members of an army of occupation by rebels for the political purpose of trying to force that army out of the rebels' own country is 'murder' equivalent to the criminal offence of taking life to fulfil a desire for sex or money or

personal revenge, but that the killing of rebels by an organised army of occupation for another political purpose –
liquidation of opposition to their presence – is not criminal.

Shortage of Statesmen

The fact is that no statesman of stature has arisen in Britain
or has held power long enough over the past twenty-two
years to bring this centuries-old war of attrition to an end,
by withdrawing British troops from the six counties. Instead,
they have chosen to stay on, in what is in fact a no win situation for them. All over the world countries similarly placed
have hauled down their flags and withdrawn their troops to
their home territories. The Soviet Union discovered after ten
years fighting the guerrillas in Afghanistan that it had no
other option but to withdraw from a war of attrition, leaving
up to a million Afghans and an undisclosed number of their
own soldiers dead behind them. In 1991, they also found
that they had to withdraw from Lithuania, Latvia and Esto-
nia. Colonial flags and troops have now been withdrawn
from India, Burma, Aden, and almost every country in Asia,
Africa and elsewhere. The Berlin Wall and the Iron Curtain
have been pulled down and millions of Russian troops have
been withdrawn to their homelands. Germany has been re-
united and other partitioned countries like Vietnam and
Korea are making moves to unite. Almost alone in the modern world, England is still maintaining her military grip on a
small bit of neighbouring territory – about the size of Yorkshire – which she forcibly annexed in 1800.

Alternatives for the Future

What the future holds for the six counties now, rests entirely
with the British. They alone have the necessary power and
arms to determine the course of events. They have really
only two alternatives open to them. They can hold on to the
area with full military force as at present, with an unwin-
nable colonial war of attrition on their hands, and without
the slightest prospect of ever seeing it end. That way surely

lie more killings, more discrimination, more oppression, more terrorism. It offers no prospect of any final solution.

Or they can decide to give up the claim to the area enshrined in the Act of Union, haul down the Union Jack and withdraw British troops from Ireland forever. That way those who live on the island of Ireland will then have to make their own arrangements for the government of Ireland on a basis that will work. The withdrawal of British forces would enable such negotiations to begin and would not mean victory for anybody or anything except reason and common sense.

There are those who argue that withdrawal would lead to even more bloodshed than exists at present. Yet, hundreds of thousands of troops have been withdrawn over recent decades from colonial involvement in other parts of the world without ensuing bloodshed. The Baltic States, Poland, East Germany, Czechoslovakia, Hungary and Bulgaria are all examples of controlled withdrawal of substantial former USSR military forces without consequent upheaval. In the final analysis, the British Government controls the British army and the billions of pounds going into the six counties every year from the British Treasury, and there is nothing to prevent them from withdrawing their troops from that area if they have the political will to do so.

Appendix

Unanimous Declaration of Dáil Éireann Adopted on the Joint Proposition of An Taoiseach, John A. Costello, and Leader of the Opposition, Eamon de Valera, on 10 May 1949:

Dáil Éireann,
Solemnly re-asserting the indefeasible right of the Irish Nation to the unity and integrity of the national territory, re-affirming the sovereign right of the people of Ireland to choose its own form of government and, through its democratic institutions, to decide all questions of national policy, free from outside interference, repudiating the claim of the British Parliament to enact legislation affecting Ireland's territorial integrity in violation of these rights, and pledging the determination of the Irish people to continue the struggle against the unjust and unnatural partition of our country until it is brought to a successful conclusion; places on record its indignant protest against the introduction in the British Parliament of legislation purporting to endorse and continue the existing partition of Ireland, and calls upon the British Government and people to end the present occupation of our six north-eastern counties, and enable the unity of Ireland to be restored and the age-long differences between the two nations brought to an end.

On the same date, Dáil Éireann directed that the above Declaration be transmitted to the Governments and the Parliaments of all countries with whom Ireland had diplomatic relations.

The foregoing resolution of Dáil Éireann represents the only declaration of policy in regard to partition adopted by Dáil Éireann since the Constitution of Ireland was enacted by the people on 1 July 1937.

Select Bibliography

Tom Barry, *Guerrilla Days in Ireland*, Anvil Books, Dublin, 1981.

Piaras Béaslaí, *Michael Collins and the Making of a New Ireland*, Volumes 1 and 2, Phoenix Publishing Co, Dublin, 1926.

Elizabeth Bowen, *Bowen's Court*, Longmans, Green & Co, London, 1942.

Andrew Boyd, *Holy War in Belfast*, Anvil Books, Dublin, 1969.

Mary Colum, *Life and the Dream*, Macmillan, London, 1947.

Tom Corfe, *The Phoenix Park Murders*, Hodder & Stoughton, London, 1968.

Daniel Corkery, *The Hidden Ireland*, M.H. Gill & Co, Dublin, 1924.

F.P. Crozier, *Ireland for Ever*, Jonathan Cape, London, 1932.

Edmund Curtis, *A History of Ireland*, Methuen & Co, London, 1936.

Edmund Curtis and R.B. McDowell (eds), *Irish Historical Documents 1172–1922*, Methuen & Co, London, 1945.

Michael Davitt, *The Fall of Feudalism in Ireland, or The Story of the Land League Revolution*, Harper & Brother, London and New York, 1904.

The Directory of Discrimination, Equality, Belfast, 1991.

Paul Dubois, *Contemporary Ireland*, Introduction by T.M. Kettle, MP, Maunsel & Co, Dublin, and Baker & Taylor, New York, 1908.

Michael Farrell, *Northern Ireland: The Orange State*, Pluto Press, London, 1976.

Michael Farrell, *Sheltering the Fugitive*, Mercier Press, Cork and Dublin, 1985.

John M. Feehan, *Bobby Sands and the Tragedy of Northern Ireland*, Mercier Press, Cork and Dublin, 1983.

Paul Foot, *Ireland: Why Britain Must Get Out*, Chatto & Windus, London, 1989.

Frank Gallagher, *The Invisible Island: The History of the Partition of Ireland*, Victor Gollancz, London, 1957.

Giraldus Cambrensis, *Historical works containing 'The Topography and the History of the Conquest of Ireland'*, Translated by Thomas Forester, George Bell & Sons, 1881.

Stephen Gwynn, *History of Ireland*, Macmillan, London, and Talbot Press, Dublin, 1924.

Handbook of the Ulster Question, North Eastern Boundary Bureau, Stationery Office, Dublin, 1923.

David Hogan, *The Four Glorious Years*, Irish Press Ltd, Dublin, 1953.

Rosamund Jacob, *The Rise of the United Irishmen*, George Harrap & Co Ltd, London, 1937.

Helen Landreth, *The Pursuit of Robert Emmet*, Richview Press, Dublin, 1949.

W.E.H. Lecky, *A History of Ireland in the 18th Century*, Volumes I–V, Longmans, Green & Co, London, 1892.

F.S.L. Lyons, *Ireland since the Famine*, Weidenfeld and Nicholson, London, 1971.

Dorothy Macardle, *The Irish Republic. A documented chronicle of the Anglo-Irish Conflict and the Partitioning of Ireland with a detailed account of the period 1916–23*, Preface by Eamon de Valera, Irish Press Publications, Dublin, 1951.

Joseph McVeigh, *A Wounded Church*, Mercier Press, Cork and Dublin, 1989.

Richard R. Madden, *The United Irishmen: Their Lives and Times*, Martin Lester Ltd, Dublin, 1923.

John Mitchel, *The History of Ireland*, Volumes 1 and 2, R & T Washbourne Ltd, London. Published c. 1869.

T.W. Moody (ed), *The Fenian Movement*, Mercier Press, Cork, 1968.

Seán Moylan, Unpublished statement, dated 6 May 1953.

Raymond Murray, *The SAS in Ireland*, Mercier Press, Cork and Dublin, 1990.

Barry O'Brien, *The Life of Charles Stewart Parnell*, T. Nelson and Son, London, 1910.

T.P. O'Connor, *The Parnell Movement*, Kegan Paul Trench & Co, London, Edinburgh, Dublin and New York, 1886.

Ernie O'Malley, *On Another Man's Wound*, Rich & Cowan, London, 1936.

Thomas Packenham, *The Year of Liberty*, Hodder & Stoughton, London, 1969.

Anna Parnell, *The Tale of a Great Sham*, Arlen House, Dublin, 1986.

'Report of the Trials of the prisoners charged with the Phoenix Park Murders, the attempt to murder Mr Field and the Conspiracy to Murder', Alex Thom & Co, Dublin, 1883.

Nora Robertson, *Crowned Harp*, Allen Figgis & Co, Dublin, 1960.

Desmond Ryan, *The Phoenix Flame*, Arthur Barker Ltd, London, 1937.

Bobby Sands, *One Day in My Life*, Mercier Press, Cork and Dublin, 1983.

Bobby Sands, *Skylark Sing Your Lonely Song*, Mercier Press, Cork and Dublin, 1989.

Claire Tomalin, *The Life and Death of Mary Wollstonecraft*, Weidenfeld and Nicholson, London, 1974; Pelican Books, 1977.

Theobald Wolfe Tone, *Life of Theobald Wolfe Tone*, Volumes 1 and 2. Published in Washington; printed by Gales and Seaton.

P.J.P. Tynan, *The Irish National Invincibles and their Times*, Chatham & Co, London, 1894.

Arthur Young, *A Tour of Ireland made by Arthur Young in the years 1776, 1777 and 1778, and brought down to the end of 1779*, London, 1780; edited by A.W. Hutton, 2 volumes, 1892; reprinted Shannon 1970.